World of Difference

World of Difference

A Moral Perspective
on Social Inequality

Compiled by Naomi Ellemers
Edited by Belle Derks,
Félice Van Nunspeet, Daan Scheepers
and Jojanneke Van der Toorn

AUP

The publication of this book was made possible by funding from the Lorentz Center (Leiden University), the Royal Netherlands Academy of Arts and Sciences (KNAW), and the NWO Spinoza grant, awarded to Naomi Ellemers.

Also published in Dutch: N. Ellemers (ed.), *Wereld van verschil. Sociale ongelijkheid vanuit een moreel perspectief* [ISBN 978 94 6298 451 6]
Translation: Gioia Marini

Cover illustration: Johnny Miller/Millefoto/Rex Shutterstock
Lay-out: Gijs Mathijs Ontwerpers

Amsterdam University Press English-language titles are distributed in the US and Canada by the University of Chicago Press.

ISBN   978 94 6298 402 8
E-ISBN   978 90 4853 454 8 (pdf)
NUR   740

Contents

Acknowledgments

This book is the result of the collaborative efforts of a multidisciplinary group of researchers. They analyzed the origins and implications of social inequality from different perspectives during a week-long workshop in May 2016, sponsored by the Lorentz Center at Leiden University. The workshop and the publication of this book were also supported by a KNAW grant awarded to Naomi Ellemers.

The essays and further content of this book were jointly prepared by the team of workshop organizers: Belle Derks, Naomi Ellemers, Félice Van Nunspeet, Daan Scheepers, and Jojanneke Van der Toorn (in alphabetical order). The essays are based on discussions during the workshop provided by all participants: Neelke Doorn, Joseph Heath, Frank Hindriks, Pauline Kleingeld, Kate Pickett, Madeleine Power, Sabine Roeser, Servaas Storm, Gwen Van Eijk, Irene Van Staveren, and Richard Wilkinson. Their expert contributions are not only included in the arguments put forth in the essays, but also in personalized text boxes elaborating specific points. The statistics and graphs, as well as the list of annotated references and reading suggestions also are the product of their collective contributions.

We gratefully acknowledge the support from the Lorentz Center, in particular Eline Pollaert who took care of all practicalities. Leon Hilbert and Lisa van Es provided valuable assistance during the workshop. Piet Groot supported us throughout the project in collecting and organizing all materials. Marjolijn Voogel from AUP enthusiastically helped us envision and realize the publication of this book.

Amsterdam, spring 2017

Authors

Belle Derks is Professor of Social and Organizational Psychology at Utrecht University. She studies how women and ethnic minorities in work and educational settings are affected by negative stereotypes, and what they themselves and organizations can do to maintain their motivation, ambition and performance.

Neelke Doorn is Associate professor of Ethics and Philosophy of Technology at the Technical University Delft. Her research concentrates on moral issues in risk governance, with a special focus on environmental risks and water security.

Naomi Ellemers is a social psychologist and Distinguished University Professor at Utrecht University. She studies how membership of social groups impacts upon individual outcomes. In her recent work she specifically focuses on the impact of morality and moral motivation.

Joseph Heath is Professor in the Department of Philosophy and the School of Public Policy and Governance at the University of Toronto. He has worked extensively in the field of critical theory, philosophy and economics, practical rationality, distributive justice, and business ethics.

Frank Hindriks is Professor of Ethics, Social and Political Philosophy at the University of Groningen. The main theme of his research is moral responsibility, investigating the attribution of praise and blame, and how people employ rationalizations to disavow responsibility.

Pauline Kleingeld is Professor of Philosophy at the University of Groningen. Her expertise centres on moral theory, Immanuel Kant and Kantian ethics, practical reason, and philosophical cosmopolitanism.

Kate Pickett is Professor of Epidemiology at the University of York, the University's Research Champion for Justice & Equality, and a Trustee of The Equality Trust. Her research focuses on the social determinants of health and health inequalities, in particular the links between income inequality, well-being and sustainability.

Madeleine Power is a researcher in public health, working on health inequalities and food insecurity in the UK. She trained in social and political sciences at Cambridge and social policy at the London School of Economics and Political Science (LSE), and has experience of conducting quantitative and qualitative research in third-sector research organizations.

Sabine Roeser is Distinguished Antoni van Leeuwenhoek Professor and head of the Ethics and Philosophy of Technology Section at the Delft University of Technology. Her research covers theoretical, foundational topics concerning the nature of moral knowledge, intuitions, emotions and evaluative aspects of risk.

Daan Scheepers is Associate professor of Social and Organizational Psychology at Leiden University. His research centres on group processes, intergroup relations (the psychology of 'us and them'), threat, and identity.

Servaas Storm is Assistant professor of Economics of Technology and Innovation at the Technical University Delft. He works on macro-economics, (induced) technological progress, income distribution and economic growth, finance, development and structural change, and climate change.

Gwen Van Eijk is Assistant professor of Criminology at the Erasmus University Rotterdam. She studies how crime control reflects and shapes class inequality.

Félice Van Nunspeet is Assistant professor of Social and Organizational Psychology at Utrecht University. She uses (implicit) behavioural and neuro-biological measures – such as EEG and fMRI – to study why and how people adhere to moral (group) norms, and which cognitive processes are associated with this motivation.

Irene Van Staveren is an economist and Professor at the International Institute of Social Studies of Erasmus University Rotterdam. Her expertise is in the intersection of economics and ethics, in particular on issues of inequality such as gender gaps, poverty, and the global divide between rich and poor countries.

Jojanneke Van der Toorn is Professor of Lesbian, Gay, Bisexual and Transgender Workplace Inclusion at Leiden University, and Assistant Professor in Social and Organizational Psychology at Utrecht University. She studies diversity in society and organizations and mainly focuses on the social psychological mechanisms involved in how, why, and when people resist, provide support for, or directly engage in social change.

Richard Wilkinson is Professor Emeritus of Social Epidemiology at the University of Nottingham Medical School, Honorary Professor at University College London and Visiting Professor at the University of York. He has played a formative role in international research on the social determinants of health and on the societal effects of income inequality.

'Income inequality is the "defining challenge of our time". ... we ... trust our institutions less (and) trust each other less when there's greater inequality'

President Barack Obama (December 4, 2013)

'Inequality is the root of social ills.'

Pope Francis (November 24, 2013)

'... the economics profession (has) downplayed inequality for too long. Now all of us have a better understanding that a more equal distribution of income allows for more economic stability, more sustained economic growth, and healthier societies with stronger bonds of cohesion and trust.'

Christine Lagarde, Director, IMF (January 23, 2013)

'Social and economic inequalities can tear the social fabric, undermine social cohesion and prevent nations from thriving. Inequality can breed crime, disease and environmental degradation and hamper economic growth.'

Ban Ki-Moon, UN Secretary General (July 9, 2013)

1

Social inequality: Myths and facts

Naomi Ellemers

Open your eyes

Life is unfair. In many large cities, opulent homes can be found right alongside poor neighbourhoods. The new medicines that pharmaceutical companies develop are so expensive that many people can't afford to use them. And while some people work all hours to get their job done, many others cannot find employment. Inequalities also characterize the lives of people in different countries. In some parts of the world, families flee hearth and home to survive; in others, people feel unsafe because they fear being burgled. Ice rinks are constructed in the middle of deserts for the entertainment of some. Yet many others are helpless in the face of natural disasters that destroy their homes and endanger the provision of food.

We can all see that social inequality exists and that it creates problems. But it is less clear what *causes* such inequality. Do

1.1

Rawls' veil of ignorance

Gwen Van Eijk en Sabine Roeser

What happens when two children have to share a cookie? It depends. Chances of getting an equal division are best when one child divides the cookie and the other is allowed to choose first. This is less likely to happen when one child divides the cookie and gives part of it away. This example illustrates the point of a famous thought experiment designed by philosopher John Rawls to explain the 'veil of ignorance'. Imagine that no one knows what his or her preferences, abilities or position in society will be – because this is covered by a veil of ignorance– what kind of society would we want to live in?

This thought experiment invites us to think about fairness, equality and justice. Those who choose to have a society that is very hard on people with few abilities or who are born into a group with a low social status, might suffer if they happen to end up as someone with few abilities or belonging to a low-status group. This way of thinking thus helps us transform self-interest into general interest. A similar principle underlies insurances: everybody contributes an equal share, not knowing who will be the one needing a smaller or larger payment or nothing at all. This justice principle can be threatened when insurances refuse to accept people who are considered high risk (e.g., because they suffer from a chronic illness), or give discounts to those who are unlikely to undergo costly medical treatments (e.g., students).

different outcomes simply reflect differences in capabilities and priorities? Do they result from diverging choices? Is it a matter of chance that some people are lucky while others suffer misfortune? So are some people often lucky while others encounter misfortune every time? How can this be? What are the consequences of these inequalities? Can they be ignored, or should we try to tackle them; and if so, how? In the public debate on social inequality different kinds of explanations are offered, for instance by journalists or politicians. Scholars who engage in this debate tend to address specific issues, or only consider their own disciplinary perspective. With all these competing analyses being put forth, it is easy to lose heart and conclude that the origins of social inequality are so complex that a solution is out of our reach. We thus tend to close our eyes to the inequality that exists, because we don't see how it could be resolved. We assume it does not matter what we do; we hope that things will be sorted out in the end, or we trust others to take care of them. These are all missed opportunities. We need to acknowledge the problems we face before we can address them, for they will not be resolved by themselves. If we do nothing, things will only get worse. Because it truly matters what we do – or fail to do.

How?

This book aims to shed new light on the debate on social inequality. We brought together academic experts from a variety of disciplines to examine this issue in depth. Throughout the book, we take a moral perspective (see Box 1.1): What is fair? What kind of world do we want to live in? By taking these questions as our starting point and combining knowledge from different academic disciplines, we evaluate the conceptions held by the public against scholarly knowledge in order to separate facts from myths.

This book captures our collective insights in an integrated analysis. The consequences of social inequality are made visible in photographs and statistics, because we have to face reality, however unpleasant it may be, instead of turning a blind eye. In this book we explain why many measures are not particularly effective, and draw on scientific knowledge to elucidate what kinds of solutions are necessary and feasible.

Resolving social inequality seems a daunting task, because it touches upon different areas of life. When we think about social inequality, we tend to focus on the differences between people, for instance in income and living standards. But such differences are closely linked to other important life outcomes (see Box 1.2), such as health and life expectancy or educational level and career opportunities. Social differences also play a role on a larger scale, for example in the movements and absorption of migrants, or in the way we use our natural habitat and deal with ecological hazards.

Common roots
Richard Wilkinson

We tend to think that inequalities in different areas – in health, education, or opportunities for children – are separate problems. They are often discussed as injustices requiring different remedial policies. But although many policies which would improve health would make little difference to education and vice versa, it is essential to recognise that most of the problems routed in relative deprivation also share some powerful common causes.

Most of the problems which within any society are more common lower down the social ladder, get worse when differences in income and wealth between rich and poor get larger. Basically, problems related to social status get worse when social status differences get bigger. As a result, countries with wider income gaps between rich and poor have higher rates of a range of social problems (such as homicide rates and level of mental illness) compared with more equal countries (see Figure 2).

This pattern is partly explained by the way bigger income differences increase the scale of relative deprivation. But although inequality has its biggest effects among the poorest, it leads to worse outcomes across all sections of society. That is because bigger income differences make class and status – social position – more important throughout society. Those with lower status are eager to climb, and those with higher status are fearful to lose their status. Status anxiety increases in all income groups and, as status competition increases, social relations, community life and our willingness to trust others declines.

In this first chapter, we examine common assumptions and popular solutions. We critically assess what tends to be seen as the main cause of social inequality, and what kind of solution this seems to require. Is this analysis well founded? Are the explanations commonly put forth substantiated by scientific facts, or are they myths that must be debunked before we can tackle the real causes of inequality?

Myths and facts

Myth 1: Economic growth is always good.

A growing economy creates many opportunities. This is most clearly visible when the starting point is highly unfavourable. In developing countries, for instance, economic growth can improve access to food, education, and health care. But where such basic provisions are already available, further economic growth can also have negative effects. There are often costs associated with economic growth; for example, because natural resources are depleted or harm is done to the environment. A singular focus on increasing a country's Global Domestic Product (GDP) can easily overlook this. In various countries, including the Netherlands, increases in GDP per capita do not necessarily improve national wellbeing, as indicated by the state of education, work, health, security, or the environment (see Figure 1). Moreover, further economic growth is often accompanied by increasing inequality. Those who already have a signifi-

1.3

Moral reasoning: For better or worse

Frank Hindriks

Morality matters to how people decide what to do. This is to a large extent because people have a desire to act in accordance with the moral norms they have adopted. And they are prone to notice discrepancies between what they want to do and their moral norms. In spite of this, people often end up acting in harmful or otherwise immoral ways. How can this be?

Even though virtually everybody engages in moral reasoning, people often do so in a self-serving manner. When they are tempted to do something harmful, they find ways of justifying the action to themselves, or to excuse or exonerate themselves. How can it be wrong to take home office supplies when 'everybody is doing it'? Sexual harassment is often justified in terms of the clothing someone wears, i.e. by 'blaming the victim'. Engaging in military combat becomes significantly easier when civilian casualties are euphemistically labelled as 'collateral damage'.

Where do things go wrong? Morality matters in that people register moral discrepancies and often feel guilty already prior to performing a harmful action. Ideally, people subsequently refrain from performing this action and change their plans so as to conform to their norms. When, however, this is not the case, they may arrive at the conclusion that, in spite of appearances, it is permitted to act in the preferred manner. What is particularly striking about such self-serving moral reasoning is that, as a consequence, people rarely believe of their own actions that they are bad. In this way, as the psychologist Albert Bandura famously noted, people are able to 'behave harmfully and still live in peace with themselves'.

cant amount of wealth and many opportunities benefit the most from economic growth, while this is rarely the case for those with little wealth and few opportunities. Without policies that level out such discrepancies, economic growth can easily induce greater inequality, which in turn is linked to a number of negative societal outcomes (see Figure 2).

In its 2014 report 'Off the Deep End', the Institute for Policy Studies noted that income disparities in the US increased during the recovery from the most recent economic crisis. On Wall Street, bonuses were already the same as or even higher than before the crisis, while the minimum wage in the US had remained unchanged in all those years. Clearly, not everyone benefited from the economic recovery.

Nowadays, more and more people are aware of these facts. And yet economic and social policies are still based on the implicit assumption that economic growth is always good. Hence, it is commonly believed that we should support companies and people that can ensure growth, for example by allowing tax exemptions or by supporting them with taxpayers' money.

Why is the myth of economic growth so persistent? Of course, in a growing economy it is easier to maintain that everyone will be better off in the end. This allows us to ignore the fact that there is a small segment of the population that clearly benefits most from a growing economy. Those who insist that growth is always good are in fact justifying

Figure 1

GDP per capita and wellbeing (the Netherlands 2003-2015)

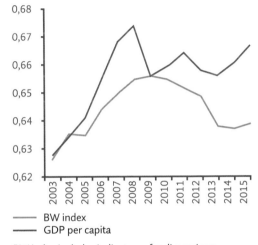

—— BW index
—— GDP per capita

BW index includes indicators of 11 dimensions indicating the state of health, safety, environment, education, income, employment and working hours, housing, civic and community engagement, following OECD taxonomy of better life index.

Source: Netherlands beyond GDP: A Wellbeing Index. Institutions for Open Societies, Utrecht University and Rabobank Economic Research. December 21, 2016.

Figure 2
Health and social problems are worse in more unequal countries

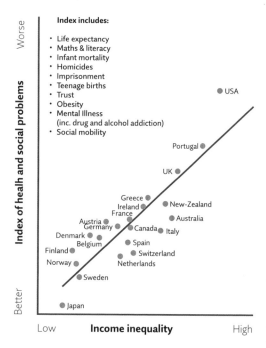

Index includes:

· Life expectancy
· Maths & literacy
· Infant mortality
· Homicides
· Imprisonment
· Teenage births
· Trust
· Obesity
· Mental Illness
  (inc. drug and alcohol addiction)
· Social mobility

Source: Wilkinson & Pickett, The Spirit Level (2009)

economic choices that leave many people worse off (see Box 1.3).

Myth 2: Equal rights provide equal opportunities.
Legally anchoring equal rights and enforcing such laws can help to curb inequality, but it is only a first step. Providing equal *rights* does not mean that people actually enjoy equal *opportunities*.

Factors such as social class, gender, and ethnicity all play a role in the opportunities that people get, regardless of their abilities, rights, or choices. When we assess people's accomplishments, we may form different expectations of their strengths and weaknesses merely because they look or speak differently than we do. We do this unintentionally and often unwittingly. Yet it can have far-reaching effects. This has repeatedly been demonstrated in studies where identical letters and CVs were submitted in response to a job vacancy. Merely changing the names of candidates resulted in a different assessment of their achievements and potential, even though the statement of their qualifications was identical.

We assess the ambitions and achievement potential of different individuals differently, simply because of who they are and where they come from. These first impressions make us more willing to give some people the benefit of the doubt, even if this is based on unfounded expectations.

We generally tend to seek, consider, and remember information that confirms our first impressions. This makes it difficult for people to prove their actual worth, especially if the first impression we have of them is not very favourable. Those who belong to a group that has had little success in society are also disadvantaged in another way. Success not only reflects *the things you can do* but also depends on *the people you know*. It is easier to show your worth when you know someone who can introduce you to relevant decision makers. It is much more difficult to convince others of your qualities if there is no one to show you the way or help you get started. The formal right to equal treatment does not compensate for this.

1.4

Mainstream economics is not value-neutral

Irene Van Staveren

The economist John Maynard Keynes wrote in 1936 that economics is a moral science. But today, most economists regard their discipline as value-free and objective. This view is defended with the distinction between economic analysis and economic policy implications: the second is considered moral, concerned with what ought to be, whereas the first is considered neutral, concerned with models, calculations, and statistical data. Economists working in the tradition of Keynes or other traditions outside the mainstream disagree with this view. We claim that economic analysis is not nor can be morally neutral.

First, *economists* are not morally neutral: recent research has shown that political attitudes of economists relate to the type of research they do and the policy advice they provide.

Second, the evaluative criterion used for markets is efficiency. This is a moral value and is concerned with the minimization of waste. The *exclusive focus on efficiency* implies neglect of other values such as equality, security or sustainability.

Third, mainstream economics assumes that all economic agents strive to *maximize their individual utility*. This implies an exclusive focus on maximum outcomes with minimum use of inputs, which should lead to efficiency in a fully competitive market context. This approach is limited because it does not allow for redistribution between agents in order to maximize aggregate utility.

Fourth, real-world economic agents often do not maximize utility – they either follow certain moral principles and social norms, or they make choices following emotions, instincts, or instructions.

Fifth, there is increasing evidence showing that efficiency and equality are not trade-offs but that a more equal distribution of resources tends to improve efficiency. Hence, policies such as free education or affordable health care insurance for all, benefit human capital and labour productivity. This leads to higher levels of income and wellbeing, which is regarded as efficient by economists of all types, and can be expressed in terms of GDP growth.

Myth 3: People only change when this benefits their self-interest.

Attempts to influence human behaviour are often guided by the assumption that people pursue economic gain. For instance, our strong faith in the blessings of the free market is based on the notion that people make rational choices aiming to maximize their profits. Government policies rely on financial incentives and sanctions to influence companies and organizations. Managers at these companies and organizations rely on similar mechanisms in guiding the behaviour of citizens, clients, and employees. All these parties are treated as separate individuals who rationally try to maximize their own outcomes and pursue their own interests. Yet many economists have identified alternative models that offer an equally valid or even superior understanding of human motivation (see Box 1.4).

The implicit assumption that people are self-interested individuals who are primarily driven by the pursuit of profit maximization also impacts on the way in which we deal with social inequality. We often tell each other that income differences are necessary in order to induce people to perform well. Reductions in welfare benefits are often justified in this way. It is assumed that the opportunity to earn more money offers an important incentive for people to seek employment. But is this the only reason why people work? If it were, how could we explain why so many people freely donate their time and efforts to do volunteer work? The importance of high earnings is also cited to justify top salaries in the corporate world. If the pay were not competitive – so it is argued – the most talented workers would move abroad. Yet we see that many talented people are reluctant to move to another country because they value other aspects of life, such as the national culture or their ties with family and friends. These examples show it is too easy to assume that people always seek economic profit and will do anything to achieve this.

At the same time, we know that there are important drawbacks to motivating people in this way. Research has established that the use of competitive incentive schemes and performance systems elicits untruthful reporting of performance results and misbehaviour. The prospect of financial gain is also seen as an important root cause in recent cases of large-scale fraud, such as the diesel-emissions software scandal or the fixing of LIBOR interest rates in banking.

What, then, would be a viable alternative to approaches based on economic profit maximization? Why do people change their behaviour if this brings them no material gain? Research reveals that there are other factors besides self-interest and rational choices that guide people's behaviour. For instance, the choices they make are also informed by their identity, by the emotions they experience, or by the motivation to do what is morally right (see Box 1.5). In different studies, the desire for *equality* emerges as a relevant concern. Common interests, similar goals, shared values and experiences, and empathy and care for each other are all strong motives that can lead people to transcend their own interests. In fact, a basic behavioural motive is implied in the need to belong and to be respected and valued by others who are important to the self (see also Box 4.4). Empathy and care are also important drivers of human be- haviour. People are willing to make all kinds of sacrifices to achieve such goals, often acting in ways that seem to make little sense or appear to be irrational. In order to under- stand this kind of behaviour, we must take into account that people cannot simply be considered individual actors who act rationally to maximize their own benefits. They are also social animals who look to each other for respect, support, and guidance.

Myth 4: Social unrest only reflects discontent over personal outcomes.
We live in an era of social unrest. Young people are eager to find work and to have their own home, but they are unable to support themselves. Migrants abandon everything they know and love in search of a better future. They end up in countries where people worry whether there are enough employment and housing opportunities for all. No wonder, then, that people rise up in protest.

1.5

Convincing people to change their moral behaviour

Naomi Ellemers and Félice Van Nunspeet

Research shows that people have a strong motivation to consider themselves as moral persons. They try to do what they consider morally right, also if this means that they have to abandon their personal preferences. The desire to be moral is a very important motive –people attempt to do what is moral, even when they know this will make them seem less friendly or less smart.

The drawback of this desire is that people find it aversive to consider the ways in which their behaviour may be lacking in morality. When we monitor their brain activity, we see that people carefully attend to their moral lapses. When we consider their physiological stress responses we see that they are quite upset by their moral shortcomings. Yet when we ask them to explain what they did, they tend to justify their behaviour, or deny its moral implications. Why? Precisely because they care so deeply about being moral, confronting people with their moral short-

comings easily induces a sense of threat and raises defensive responses. Hence, insisting that their behaviour is lacking in morality may not be the most productive way to get people to *change*. It only makes them unhappy, hostile, and defensive.

How can we use this knowledge to convince people to change their moral behaviour? Feelings of threat are alleviated when people are explicitly invited to *improve* their moral behaviour. Asking them to focus on the moral ideals and possible solutions to achieve these, helps them engage and plan for ways to be more effective in doing what they consider to be morally right.

Further, people are most likely to do what is moral when their behaviour is monitored by others who are important to them. They hope to earn respect and social inclusion by acting in ways that are morally approved by these others.

On the surface, it would seem that the forces driving social unrest and political protest relate to people's frustrations about their own outcomes and prospects in life. For example, the people who joined the 'Occupy Wall Street' movement described themselves as 'the 99 per cent'. This was intended to emphasize the distinction between the majority of people and the richest one per cent in the US, who earn disproportionately more than the rest.

But other indications suggest that income disparities are not the main reason that people revolt. Indeed, the Occupy movement was not only directed at differences in income, but also at the disproportionate *influence* that the richest one per cent have on politics. People protested against the fact that the interests, wishes, and preferences of such a small group dictate the systems we develop (or fail to develop) to work together, live together, and show solidarity in caring for each other. Even those who benefit from current arrangements can see that for many people, the system is not working. The protests that are voiced also reflect such broader concerns and moral ideals.

A case in point is the attitude towards migrants. Countering common beliefs, research shows that the reluctance to accommodate more migrants is *not* primarily driven by individual concerns over economic outcomes. As we will see in Chapter 4, attitudes towards migrants mainly relate to uncertainties about our ability to deal with cultural differences, instead of

1.6

Identity threats and the stability of social hierarchies

Daan Scheepers

Why is it so difficult to reduce social inequality? Research has addressed the role of (physiological) threat implied by the prospect of change.

This work shows that when power differences are *stable*, the powerless show signs of threat. They display a maladaptive pattern of high blood pressure, accompanied by high vascular resistance, and low cardiac performance. When power differences are *unstable*, similar threat is shown by those in power. This helps to explain why people in power may be reluctant to reduce social inequality. For them, social change implies losing their privileged position.

These dynamics not only play out at the individual level, but also at the group level. They are visible not only when 'real' material resources are at stake but also when status differences are more symbolic.

This is not always evident from what people say. Physiological signs of threat to unstable status relations may emerge even among those who endorse egalitarian views. For instance, when discussing changing gender roles in society, males showed increased blood pressure, especially when discussing this with a woman. However, under these circumstances their endorsement of explicit sexist statements was reduced. Thus surface level openness to social change can co-occur with the experience of threat, which may impede the propensity to engage in *real* action towards changing gender roles.

Is there hope? Research shows that members of dominant groups *can* become positively engaged by the prospect of social change. Both their explicit attitudes and their physiological responses indicate they feel positively challenged by the possibility of change, provided that they see such change as a *real* ideal, rather than as a moral obligation. Emphasizing the moral ideals underlying the desire for social change may therefore be key to achieving this.

reflecting a sense of competitiveness about economic resources. The notion that migrants have other moral values
is what people find the most disturbing; in general, people
believe that such differences in important values are difficult to reconcile. Accordingly, they fear that the influx of migrants will call into question moral values that are important
to them, and will alter the principles that govern society. In
developed countries, more abstract concerns such as these
constitute the main cause of social unrest (see also Figure 7).

From problems to solutions
Although having some form of social inequality is inevitable,
it is still worth considering the causes of such inequality, as
well as its consequences. Once we recognize that commonly held assumptions are in fact myths, we gain a different
perspective. Taking a novel perspective to examine familiar problems yields a different level of understanding and
brings to the fore other types of solutions.
Debunking common myths is important; it causes us to ask
different questions and to examine novel solutions.
If economic growth is not the silver bullet that many people
consider it to be, we need to look further. This allows us to
examine what choices are actually being justified by prior-
itizing economic growth. Who is rooting for this, and why?
We have also argued that equal rights only constitute a first
step towards creating equal opportunities. If this is the case,

1.7

Morality and unjust inequality

Neelke Doorn and Pauline Kleingeld

This book takes a moral perspective on social inequality. This prompts the immediate question what morality is. Morality refers to the set of most fundamental rules and values that provide guidance on how one ought to act. Different ethical theories take different points of departure to articulate the relevant criteria. According to some theories, the criterion for right action is formulated in terms of the *outcomes* of one's actions; according to others, what matters most is that one acts on the right underlying *principles*. The first type of theory is called 'consequentialist', the second 'deontological'. For consequentialist theories, an act is considered right if it leads to better overall outcomes, for example if the well-being of people improves. In a deontological framework, an act is right if it is in accordance with a good principle or an appropriate value. Although consequentialist and deontological theories are fundamentally different, they may overlap when it comes to concrete duties. For example, leading consequentialist and deontological theories hold that individuals have a moral duty to help people in need and to promote general well-being.

Both consequentialist and deontological theories may consider social inequality as undesirable or wrong. From a consequentialist perspective, if reducing inequality improves the total amount of well-being, inequality should be reduced. From a deontological perspective, reducing inequality may be required because equality itself is considered of value, for example, or because an equal distribution is considered more fair. Not all moral theorists regard all forms of social inequality as necessarily unjust, since some inequalities may be the result of genuinely voluntary decisions (for example, a personal preference to adopt a minimalist lifestyle). Thus, morality requires us to reduce *unjust* inequalities. This book explores what different inequalities may be at stake in the different domains and which ones should be considered unjust.

we must ask ourselves what we can do to offer everyone the same opportunities, instead of simply attributing different outcomes to individual choices and achievements – as we so often do.

And if people not only seek to differentiate themselves from others, but also have the desire to belong, this may be used to help them change their behaviour.

Finally, it helps to know that social unrest also reflects people's anxieties about the threat they experience to the *values* that are important to them, and to the moral principles they endorse. This knowledge implies that we should not consider economic outcomes alone, but that we also need to reassure people about the moral implications of current developments in society.

The structure of this book

The chapters in this book address the causes and consequences of social inequality by taking an often-overlooked perspective that goes beyond individualistic economic approaches. We view individuals as part of a collective or as members of a social group. We also consider the possibility that some groups have an interest in the maintenance of social inequality, while others aim to reduce it (see Box 1.6). In performing this exercise, we examine the added value of taking a *moral* perspective. Key questions are whether people are treated equally, and if not, whether we can arrive at a more equitable distribution by using the power of moral arguments – i.e., the desire to do the right thing (see Box 1.7). The first two chapters focus on the novel insight this perspective yields into the way in which inequality impacts on *education* and *work*. We also consider the effects that inequality can have on our *health*. The inequality between various groups in society is discussed in the chapter on *migration*. In the final chapter, we examine how taking a moral perspective changes the way we consider the inequality between different parts of the world with regard to the causes and effects of *climate change*.

For each of these subjects, we examine the added value of taking a moral perspective. When each of us pursues our own interests, this does not make the world a better place for everyone. Increasing the inequalities between people living together in the same society carries significant costs and introduces risks that affect us all. We examine the implicit mechanisms that play a role in this process. In turn, these illustrate that the use of economic incentives that make people optimize their own outcomes does not resolve the problems identified here. The only way to combat social inequality is to recognize that opportunities are not the same for everyone. Only when we ask ourselves how we can ensure that everyone is treated fairly can we begin to understand what we need to do.

2

Education and work

Jojanneke Van der Toorn

Inequality in the labour force has many faces. Ethnic minorities find it more difficult than ethnic majorities to get jobs, and are overrepresented in low-paying sectors. Women struggle to advance to higher positions at work, and on average still earn much less than men for doing the same work (approximately 16% less in the European Union and 20% less in the United States). Those with a lower level of education are more often unemployed than those with a higher level of education; the employment potential of elderly people and people with a functional impairment remains under-utilized; and sexual minorities feel less included in the workplace than heterosexuals. These kinds of differences can also be seen in education. Ethnic minorities and children from lower socio-economic backgrounds perform less well than their counterparts from higher socio-economic backgrounds and are less likely to move on to higher education. Girls are less likely to be trained in technical professions. And those who believe that measures designed to

2.1

Pay differences

Irene Van Staveren

Why do some people earn so much more than others? The difference is due to several factors. Firstly, we tend to think that people should be compensated for the additional time and effort invested in training; if you go to school longer, your subsequent income should reflect the income you were not able to earn during that time. However, many professions earn wages that are disproportional to these opportunity costs. A second factor relates to the supply and demand for certain jobs. Due to socialization, expectations, and pre-selection into stereotypical educational fields, labour markets are segmented leaving some groups with a very narrow choice of jobs and few career opportunities. For example, the majority of working women in most countries can be found in just three jobs: teacher, nurse and secretary. This oversupply pushes the wages down in these professions. A third factor relates to artificially created scarcity. Various top-professions have limited supply due to rationing in the educational system, for example by setting a limit to the number of students allowed in medical school, or due to professional entry barriers, for example by enforcing a bar exam to become a lawyer. A fourth factor has to do with status differences between job types. High status jobs tend to have high earnings, which are not clearly justified by the underlying productivity. For example, Beyoncé makes many times more money than an equally talented singer who works the same hours, but who simply has not made it and sings in small clubs for a meagre income. This is referred to as the 'winner-takes-all effect', whereby the majority of earnings accrue to those at the top and little is left for others. Even though the relationship between effort and labour output is weak, we do not question pay differences between people. Instead, we admire the rich and blame the poor, thus justifying inequality.

empower these disadvantaged groups have been reversing these trends are in for a rude awakening: social and economic inequalities between these groups is growing within different societies across the entire world.

Individual responsibility and the 'business case'

In the public debate on social inequality, it is widely recognized that inequality in education and work occurs along group lines. Newspapers are full of reports on the unequal outcomes between groups in society such as the glass ceiling, the wage gap, and ethnic minorities' lack of success in the labour market. But the explanations given for these forms of inequality tend to focus on the individual. We are inclined to look for the causes of inequality in the personal choices, qualities, and behaviour of those who are disadvantaged. Some people argue that ethnic minorities are unmotivated, do not speak the language well, or do not have the right qualifications, and that women lack leadership skills or prioritize the family. In this way, individuals are held responsible for their group's deprivation.

An often-heard argument is that these people could achieve anything if they really wanted to, because nothing stands in their way. This reflects our strong belief in society as a 'meritocracy' in which each individual's social position is determined purely by his or her own merits. In addition, we assume that people exercise great influence on the course

2.2

Myth of equal opportunities

Gwen Van Eijk

One argument to justify existing social inequality is that opportunities for socioeconomic success and mobility are equal for all. Unequal outcomes would reflect different efforts: everyone in principle has the same starting point, but some work harder than others and end up earning more income, for example, than others who work less hard. This argument is grounded in a belief that our society is meritocratic: people are rewarded based on their merits, not their social background. We find such beliefs in cultural narratives about, for example, the 'American Dream' and stories that express admiration for the 'self-made man' and those who make it 'from rags to riches.' However, such beliefs and narratives obscure the fact that opportunities are not equally distributed. Opportunities for socioeconomic success and mobility still partly depend on the socioeconomic status of people's parents (e.g. their occupational, educational or income level). Children of higher-educated and higher-earning parents on average do better than children of lower-educated and lower-earning parents. Parents who have more education, income and other valuable resources are able to invest more or in different ways in their children, in such a way that benefits their socioeconomic achievement. Intergenerational mobility is more limited and the role of class is more pronounced than we tend to think. Thus, inequality in outcomes is related to inequality in opportunities, not only in very unequal societies such as the United States but also in relatively egalitarian societies such as the Netherlands. Studies furthermore show that intergenerational mobility is more difficult in more unequal countries (this has been called 'The Great Gatsby Curve'), and that mobility becomes more difficult when inequality in a country increases because people from underprivileged backgrounds have to overcome more barriers to gain socioeconomic success.

of their lives and that factors such as ethnicity, gender, or sexual preference play little or no role in this. This way of thinking reflects a strong belief in the possibility of moving up in the world ('from newspaper boy to millionaire!'). We prefer to believe this because it allows us to be proud of our own achievements if things are going well, and to remain hopeful for a better future if things are not going well. But the downside of this is that people who are less successful get the blame for their lack of success. Do you have a low-paying job? Then you probably made the wrong choices in life and did not do your best at school.

Likewise, when it comes to solutions, the arguments are often based on this way of thinking in terms of individual choices and responsibilities. The Dutch prime minister Mark Rutte recently claimed that the solution to the problem of discrimination against ethnic minorities in the labour market lies with ethnic minorities themselves: 'You have to fight your way in.' Another example is the often-heard suggestion that if men earn more than women for the same work, women should work on improving their salary negotiation skills. And for other disadvantaged groups as well, the following mottos have become all too familiar: work harder, don't complain, and combat prejudice by proving your critics wrong.

One popular way to combat inequality in the labour market is to put more emphasis on one's *own responsibility*, especially in obtaining a good education. We often assume

Figure 3
Relative likelihood of unemployment

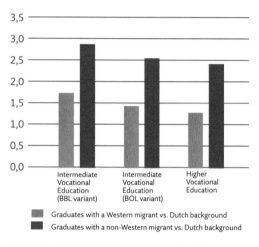

Source: ROA (2016), Schoolverlaters tussen Onderwijs en Arbeidsmarkt, ROA-R-2016/2

that there is a direct link between education and remuneration: we believe that more knowledge will get you a better job (but see Box 2.1). Education is thus seen as the key to success. This idea stems from our belief in progress combined with a strong faith in the knowledge-based economy, where knowledge workers are more valued and better paid than those in artisan trades or service occupations – even though one might question whether that is fair.

Alongside this emphasis on the individual, an *instrumental approach* is often used to try to reduce inequality in education and in the labour market. This approach stresses the importance of diversity and points out the gains that can be reaped by giving more women and minorities access to education and work. The famous 'business case' for diversity, for example, states that companies are financially better off with a diverse workforce, because diverse teams are more creative and more productive.

Unequal opportunities

The current debate thus focuses on individual and instrumental factors that explain intergroup inequality in education and work, and these factors are used to come up with solutions. But if we take a closer look, we see that it is impossible to speak of genuinely equal opportunities. For example, someone from an ethnic minority background is more likely to be unemployed than a native Dutch person, even if they both received the same education (see Figure 3). One's ethnicity and social background partly determines one's success in education and work. Thus the image of a meritocracy in which everyone is able to fully realize his or her individual potential is incorrect. This calls for solutions that not only focus on individual choices and capabilities, but that also take into account the differences between these groups in society and the opportunities they receive.

The relationship between group membership and success in education and work

The idea that obtaining a good education leads to better outcomes is not entirely true. Some people become millionaires without having followed any specific training; for example, by taking over the family business or becoming pop stars or models. Others put an enormous amount of energy into their education and development, but are unable to find a good job. These differences cannot be solely ascribed to individual factors. The correlation between obtaining higher education and making more effort on the one hand and success in the labour market on the other is far from perfect. Moreover, this relationship is less strong for certain groups than it is for others. Different groups in society clearly have differing opportunities to enter higher education, to land a better-paid job, or to end up in a prestigious profession (see also Box 2.2).

2.3

Equal opportunities in markets are dynamic

Irene Van Staveren

Markets have an inherent tendency towards unequal outcomes, and not all such inequalities are unfair. For example, if two persons with the same education earn different incomes because the one works long weeks whereas the other prefers more leisure time, the ensuing income difference is a consequence of their acting upon different goals in life. But there are other mechanisms at play as well that prevent equal opportunity from ensuring a minimum acceptable level of equality of outcomes. There are various reasons for this. A first reason is luck: some people are lucky in terms of certain talents or physical resources. Markets reward any source of resources, irrespective of whether these were obtained through luck or effort. Second, markets function on the basis of competition which is about winning. Competitive behaviour does not encourage cooperation with or help to disadvantaged groups. To the contrary, and this is the third reason why markets tend to increase inequality, strategic behaviour results in alliances by the most privileged individuals. They can lobby for regulations in their favour and in collusion between firms to win over other firms. Over time, even a fully free, competitive market, thus has a tendency to end up as an oligopoly including a few firms with the power to keep prices high and to put up barriers for potential new competitors. A fourth and final reason why markets tend towards increased inequality is through the accumulation of advantage, which in turn allows for higher risk taking and more buffers against uncertainty. The flip side of this is the accumulation of disadvantage by those with less talent, fewer resources, lower schooling, and worse health conditions. Since equal opportunity in a market setting does not prevent increasing inequality in outcomes, markets require continuous corrections in terms of redistribution, regulation, and public goods in order to prevent high levels of inequality.

2.4

Early childhood interventions

Kate Pickett

Across the political spectrum, people agree that children should have equal opportunities in life, equal chances to realise their capabilities. But to claim equal opportunity and social mobility as a guiding principle whilst ignoring income inequality is futile. Research consistently shows that children of poorer families have multiple disadvantages from birth onwards. They are more likely to have low birth weight or be born too soon, more likely to have ill health or developmental delays, less likely to be ready for school or to achieve well. If life is a race, some children are born with weights chained to their legs. In the UK Millennium Cohort Study, children who had been slow to develop their motor skills at nine months old were significantly more likely to have fallen behind in their cognitive development and were more likely to be less well behaved at age five. Poor children were almost a year behind middle class children by the time they started school. This isn't because poor parents don't care about nurturing their children's development –but inequality increases pressures on parents, increasing mental health problems, drug and alcohol use, long working hours, family tensions, and debt. Investment in early childhood programmes and support for new families can help to disrupt the intergenerational transmission of disadvantage, but much better would be to reduce the inequality that continuously creates such problems. International comparisons also clearly show that child wellbeing is significantly lower in more unequal countries, and among rich, developed countries where inequality has been increasing in recent years, child wellbeing has been declining.

2.5

How group-based stereotypes restrict the opportunities of individuals

Belle Derks

In public discourse the underrepresentation of certain groups in work and education (e.g. underrepresentation of women in leadership or STEM fields, ethnic minorities in higher education) is often attributed to the different choices people make, or differences in interest or ability. However, psychological research has revealed the significant impact that group-based stereotypes have on the ability of people targeted by these stereotypes to reach their optimal potential and the choices they make.

The stereotypes that exist in society concerning gender (women are family-oriented; men are career-oriented), race (e.g., racial differences in intelligence) or sexual orientation (e.g., gay men are effeminate) affect people belonging to these groups in several ways.

Firstly, stereotypes shape people's perception. Importantly they do so without us being consciously aware. For example, because stereotypes imply that women have lower leadership qualities than men, a woman needs to show more evidence of high ability than a man to be deemed equally qualified for a leadership position.

Secondly, in the case of gender specifically, stereo-

types may even act as norms. Women who act in a dominant way or men who show emotions not only challenge our expectations, they go against what we deem appropriate. As a result, women and men who step out of their gender role are evaluated very negatively (e.g. a woman leader is 'bossy'). As such, gender stereotypes are a powerful force that motivate women and men to act in line with their social role (e.g. women reducing working hours after having a child). Finally, through a process called 'stereotype threat' stereotypes can directly reduce the motivation and performance of people who are targets of stereotypes. A large body of experimental research shows that reminding people about negative stereotypes – be it blatantly (making a joke about women's lack of mathematical ability) or subtly (asking Black students to record their race on an intelligence test) – directly limits cognitive abilities because it triggers negative emotions that take up working memory resources. Moreover, over time the stress of stereotype threat erodes people's motivation, leading them to disengage from domains in which they are negatively stereotyped and choose domains in which they do not face the burden of disproving a negative stereotype.

According to the Organization for Economic Co-operation and Development (OECD), a person's success in education and work is correlated with his or her parents' socio-economic background, including their income. Children from low-income families are less likely to be able to afford the costs of going to university, even if they are smart enough to get in. Parents with more money can help their children receive a good education even if they are not so proficient at learning, by paying for tutors or for exam training. Even in countries where everyone has free access to good education, such as in the Netherlands, parental income level still has an influence on a child's success.

These differences between groups in society mean that some people must overcome all kinds of obstacles in their education and career, while others are more likely to get a helping hand along the way. Even if the individual advantages and disadvantages are not particularly significant, they accumulate over time. Those who receive more resources and support can afford to take more risks or build up a buffer against periods of uncertainty. This makes it easier for them to take advantage of new opportunities. But those who are just getting by – because they have less talent, money, or education, or are in poorer health – are unable to do this (see Boxes 2.3 and 2.4). This phenomenon is called the 'Matthew effect': people who are better off receive more opportunities time after time, enabling small differences to

increase over time. Even if opportunities are equal on paper, in practice they are often unequal because stereotypes influence our expectations and colour our perceptions.

Stereotyping and prejudice

Everyone tends to use generalized notions about a group in order to assess individuals from that group. Although this kind of *stereotyping* allows us to make a complex world more comprehensible, it also leads to *prejudice* that can sometimes be far removed from reality. Stereotypes colour our perceptions. The children of less educated parents, for example, are more likely to be referred to lower secondary school tracks, even if they do well in school. If Fatima makes a mistake, we tend to think that she is unable to do the task, but if Sophie makes a mistake, we assume that she was not concentrating. Even if someone does better than expected, stereotypes can work against them: female managers who act like managers are considered bossy and are negatively evaluated, while the same behaviour in male managers is rated positively. And finally, the realization that others have negative expectations of a particular group can undermine the performance of individual members of that group. This is called *stereotype threat* (see Box 2.5).

Not only *explicit,* but also *implicit* preconceptions can haunt members of ethnic groups, women, or sexual minorities. This is often more problematic because people are una-

2.6

Gendered preferences: A matter of nature *and* nurture

Sabine Roeser

Women are still disadvantaged in the workplace compared to men: they earn less for the same job and are less likely to achieve higher positions. Besides the gender bias that they face, women also contribute to gender inequality by making different career and family choices than men. What are the causes of these differences?

Difference feminism states that women are simply different from men and therefore want different things; these differences should be celebrated and re-valued. For example, caring for children and family members should be valued as much as a career outside the home. Liberal feminists agree that this may indeed help us overcome certain forms of inequality, but warn us that we should not too readily assume that women really want different things than men. Rather, our culture creates and perpetuates such strong expectations and role models, that our preferences, desires, and aspirations follow suit.

There is a lot of evidence that gender roles are to a large extent socially constructed. Ideas about what women and men are like, tend to vary a lot across space and time and thus cannot be defined without reference to the cultural and historical context. Also, women differ a lot from each other in what they want in life. Furthermore, many women have deviated from society's expectations which should remind us that there is not one definition of what it is to be a woman.

Gender differences result from nature *and* nurture. Striving for gender equality, however, does not mean that everyone has to be the same. Rather, it can mean that people are provided with the opportunity to develop in a way that suits them, independently of their sex or gender. This means that we should resist gendered expectations and make no assumptions about men's and women's career and family choices.

ware that it is happening, and because it can influence the behaviour of people who are genuinely trying to treat everyone equally. Implicit biases primarily influence assessments in ambiguous and complex situations in which people rely on their gut instinct as well as the general impression they have of the other person.

This has been identified in research on interviews in which a White job interviewer assesses a Black candidate. An interviewer who feels less at ease with a Black candidate tends unconsciously to exhibit less encouraging non-verbal behaviour. For example, the interviewer may make less eye contact or give the candidate less time to answer questions. This leads to a so-called *self-fulfilling prophecy* in which the candidate feels less at ease, affecting his or her self-presentation and thereby confirming the interviewer's negative expectations. Research has shown that these kinds of unconscious processes cause members of under-represented groups to under-perform in all sorts of school and work-related situations.

In the long term, exposure to stereotypical expectations and implicit prejudice can result in people becoming less motivated or adjusting their ambitions to the opportunities that they find (see Box 2.6). If girls hear often enough that engineering is for men, they will be less inclined to choose a technical profession. These more or less invisible processes contribute to the perpetuation of inequality by members of privileged groups as well as members of disadvantaged groups.

The paradox of equality

On the one hand, research clearly shows that equal abilities, efforts, and achievements can still lead to different outcomes as a result of the accumulation of small advantages or disadvantages generated by stereotypical expectations. On the other hand, many of our attempts to treat people equally are based on the assumption that we are capable of assessing individual merits and opportunities in an objective manner. In some cases, the conviction that this is possible can even make the situation worse. If organizations, for example, emphasize individual achievements and declare themselves to be open to diversity, managers are more inclined to believe that they are objective in their assessments. This, in turn, makes them less alert to the possibility that stereotypical expectations may be colouring their judgement, as a result of which employees actually suffer more from implicit biases. This is called the 'paradox of equality'.

All in all, there are enough indications that in order to eliminate inequality in the labour market, it is not enough simply to open up educational opportunities to disadvantaged groups. At every stage of a career, stereotypes and prejudice continue to affect the opportunities that an individual gets to demonstrate what they are capable of and the remuneration they receive for their achievements.

The selection and valuing of professions

There is a big difference in the value and remuneration attached to different professions, even for professions that require the same level of education. A job with government, for example, does not pay as much as a similar job in the corporate world. Ethnic minorities and women are over-represented in the service sector and the public sector, and more men can be found in technical positions and in the corporate world. This partly explains the difference in salaries between men and women, but individuals have less freedom to select a particular profession or sector than may at first seem to be the case. People select precisely those professions in which they expect to be successful and can get hired, because they fit the stereotype of their particular group.

Women more often choose a part-time job or make do with a job without significant career prospects because they are expected to take on the major responsibility for caring for the family. Jobs in which women are over-represented are systematically valued less and are less well paid than jobs that are dominated by men. This has little to do with the characteristics or the demands of the job. As the number of women entering a particular profession increases, there is a decline in the status and salary of that profession, a phenomenon known as 'Sullerot's law'. This is certainly the case in the health care sector, or in the Dutch judiciary.

A moral perspective

Opportunities in education and in the labour market are thus not only determined by one's own merits. Society requires the same achievements from people facing different circumstances, and the choices that people are given are limited by the fact that they belong to a certain group. This is partly the result of unconscious processes that are perpetuated by both privileged and disadvantaged groups. What are the implications of this if we want to reduce inequality? It is not enough for us simply to realize that different groups attain differing levels of success in education and work. For one thing, people tend to rationalize inequality. We like to believe that the world around us is fair and we therefore close our eyes to injustice (see also Box 4.2). Second, the way in which implicit bias works is often unconscious and unintentional. The effects of implicit prejudice therefore cannot be eradicated by simply deciding that everyone deserves to be treated equally. Third, it is particularly painful for us to face our own shortcomings when we fail to behave according to the moral values that we hold dear – such as fair treatment for all (see also Boxes 1.3 and 1.5). It is easier to focus on what appears to be fair at the individual level rather than what is unfair at the group level (see also Box 3.2).

Equality versus equity

Even when it is clear that *something* must be done, this does not indicate *what* should be done or who should do it. Should the government impose rules or should we leave it to employers? Should the solution be anonymous job applications or policies targeting certain groups?

In order to answer these questions, we need to make a distinction between equality and equity. The difference between these two concepts lies in the focus on the *starting position* in which people find themselves (see Figure 4). If we treat everyone in the same manner, we ignore the unequal starting position of different groups and the unequal obstacles that stand in their way. This means that they do not in fact enjoy equal opportunities, as shown in the upper side of Figure 4. Unequal treatment is therefore sometimes necessary in order to offer people equivalent opportunities, as shown in the lower side of Figure 4. This is the idea behind proactive measures such as affirmative action policies that target particular groups. To decide what is needed in order to be able to offer everyone equal opportunities, we must first map out the visible and less visible obstacles that exist, and pinpoint who is encountering these obstacles.

Figure 4

Equality vs. equity

Equality

Equity

What can you do?

If certain conditions were met, equal opportunities in education and the labour market would be achievable. First, we must recognize that access to education is *not sufficient* to reduce inequality in the labour market. Second, we need to ask ourselves whether the 'choices' that people make reflect their own wishes or are the result of *stereotypical expectations*. And third, we must focus on the *causes* of unequal opportunities instead of tackling their consequences. If people were given a more equal starting position at the beginning of their career, they would be better able to take advantage of the opportunities that arise. Then there would be less need for retrospective compensatory measures, which many people consider to be unfair. Investing in the development of children in their early years offers the best prospect of preventing the cycle of deprivation from being passed from generation to generation (see also Box 2.4).

If we were thereby able to increase the success of minority groups in the labour market, this would also eventually reduce the explicit and implicit prejudice against these groups. In the short term, this requires clear choices, a willingness to invest in the future, and careful communication. Affirmative action policies will be viewed as unfair preferential treatment as long as it remains unclear what kinds of obstacles these target groups face. Citing instrumental arguments such as the 'business case for diversity' as the most important motivation behind such policies is a risky approach. This suggests that there is a gain to be made in the short term. Increasing diversity is a question of patience and perseverance, however, and may initially involve significant costs. We may expect more support for a diversity policy that is motivated by moral arguments. People are often willing to do what is right in a broader social, historical, and moral context, even if they do not benefit from it directly. Current debates about inequality in education and work tend to emphasize individual choices and responsibilities, even when group memberships limit their opportunities to be successful in their education or professional career. To create truly equal opportunities, it is important to take into account moral concerns that would argue for group-level solutions.

3

Health

Félice Van Nunspeet

The consequences of social inequality are manifold. In this chapter, we examine the consequences of inequality for mental and physical health. In countries with wide income disparities, residents are generally in poorer physical and mental health than their counterparts in more equal countries (see Figure 5). And within such countries, it is primarily those with a lower level of education and lower incomes who have adverse health outcomes. On average, they lead more unhealthy lives than people with a higher level of education and higher incomes. In addition, people with a lower social status are sick more frequently and have a lower life expectancy. People with low incomes and education are at a clear disadvantage when it comes to their health. But *why* is this the case?

Health as a personal choice
We are inclined to attribute differences in health primarily to individual behaviour (see Box 3.1) and to see health as each

Figure 5.1

Infant mortality rates are higher in more unequal countries

Figure 5.2

The prevalence of mental illness is higher in more unequal rich countries

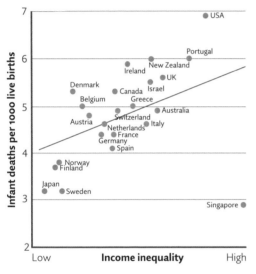

Source: Wilkinson & Pickett, The Spirit Level (2009)

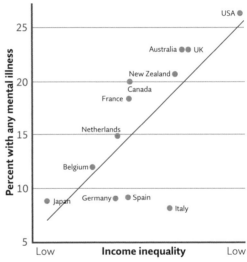

Source: Wilkinson & Pickett, The Spirit Level (2009)

person's own responsibility. People are encouraged to eat less sugar and fat, to exercise more, to refrain from smoking, and to drink less alcohol. Health policies are often focused on informing people about what constitutes a healthy or unhealthy lifestyle and convincing them to change their behaviour. Financial incentives are often used to encourage people to change their habits. For example, the government levies high taxes on alcohol and cigarettes, and medical care in many countries has a deductible. Sometimes health insurance premiums are even tailored to a person's individual health behaviour.

We assume that financial incentives help people to make the right (healthy) choices, because they allow people to weigh up the costs and benefits of their unhealthy behaviour. This approach is in line with the idea that everyone is essentially free and should be free to make their own choices. Measures to 'protect people from themselves' are sometimes seen as unwarranted government interference.

But the financial incentives that are used do not work for everyone in the same way. Making medical care more expensive mainly affects people with little disposable income. Higher costs could cause people with lower incomes to avoid available health care or not buy prescribed medicines, which would in turn result in larger health problems. And paradoxically enough, the impact of raising the price of cigarettes to reduce smoking turns out to be smaller among

Figure 5.3

More adults are obese in more unequal rich countries

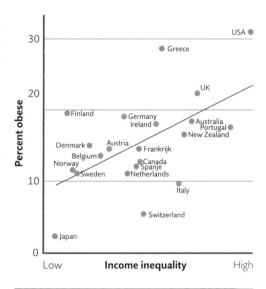

Source: Wilkinson & Pickett, The Spirit Level (2009)

people who have financial concerns, because those who do not have enough money experience financial stress, making it more difficult to stop smoking even when smoking becomes more expensive. Thus we could ask ourselves whether healthy behaviour is a personal choice, or whether people on lower incomes simply lack freedom of choice (see Box 3.2).

Large-scale government interventions to reduce health disparities are also often justified on the basis of economic arguments such as cost-benefit analyses, which point out why the financial investments that are required now could prevent higher health care costs in the long term. But given the above, it is questionable whether this is the most effective approach. There are other arguments that can be used to justify investment in health care. After all, how fair is it to dismiss health disparities as a matter of personal responsibility?

One's own fault?

If we consider all the behaviours that affect a person's health, it is debatable how many of these behaviours are genuinely free choices. After all, the way people behave also depends on the circumstances they face and the opportunities these circumstances offer them.

Based on ethnic or socio-economic differences, for example, people live in different locations, work in different jobs and companies, and spend their free time in different ways.

Lifestyle drift
Kate Pickett

In the UK, commissions into health inequalities have made recommendations to improve public health by closing the health gap between rich and poor and by policies directed towards reducing health inequalities. But these policies have failed: the gap is actually growing. Despite the research evidence that suggests we need to tackle the wider social determinants of health (e.g., income, unemployment, poverty, inequality), policy emphasis on individual lifestyle dominates. Lifestyle drift – the tendency to recognize the need for action on 'upstream' social determinants of health inequalities only to drift 'downstream' to focus largely on individual lifestyle factors (such as smoking, drinking, diet, exercise) – fits with political narratives of individual choice and responsibility. Associated with this is a move away from action to address the social gradient towards activities targeted at the most disadvantaged groups. The result is a personalization of morbidity and narratives of blame: individual choices damage our health, while health inequalities and the social injustice and health effects of poverty are neglected.

3.2

The responsibility paradox

Frank Hindriks

Each of us has to contribute her fair share. People who do not do this are not entitled to benefits that the others have generated – at least not when they did not make an effort. Furthermore, people are not entitled to help or assistance when they fail to contribute themselves. It may well be that this conception of fairness is as such impeccable. However, it is often applied in a way that has pernicious consequences.

Suppose you are unemployed, obese, or otherwise disadvantaged. People may conclude from the fact that you are impaired in one of these ways that you did something wrong. They are encouraged to do so in contexts that put a lot of emphasis on individual responsibility. In such an environment, people easily blame others for whatever disadvantage they suffer from.

Applying the logic of responsibility just described is dangerous and can have paradoxical effects. Often people are impaired by factors that are beyond their control. For instance, someone might be unemployed because he is discriminated against, perhaps due to his ethnic background or sexual orientation. If too much emphasis is put on individual responsibility, even such a person ends up being blamed for the position he is in. Or if not blamed, he might feel guilty for not measuring up to the standards set by society. After all, he does not contribute, so he must have done something wrong.

In order to avoid blaming people in insulting and debilitating ways, it is vital to appreciate the importance of collective responsibility. The logic of individual responsibility works only when background conditions are fair – for instance, when people are not discriminated. Achieving this requires shared action, and, for instance, a willingness to mutually correct each other's behaviour. The upshot is that the logic of individual responsibility can be applied properly only once people have taken their collective responsibility.

This results in different living conditions. People with a better education, a better career, and a higher income have the option of living more spaciously – on the outskirts of the city, for example – because they not only have enough money to pay for a larger house, but they can also afford to buy a car to drive to their work. Those who do not have enough money live in relatively cheap, densely-populated neighbourhoods – in the centre of the city or even in 'ghettos' of flats in unattractive suburbs.

Living conditions that have a positive influence on health (clean air, sporting facilities, a selection of fresh and healthy food, leisure activities) are thus more easily accessible for privileged groups than for groups at the bottom of the social pyramid (see also Box 5.1). In other words, there is a physical separation between different groups of people due to where they live and the facilities (including health care facilities) that are available to them. This serves to perpetuate the differences in circumstances and lifestyle that are crucial for health. Even in adjacent neighbourhoods within a city, this leads to different health outcomes.

Decisions made by government institutions and companies also constrain the choices that people can make with regard to their health. To whom is housing in a particular neighbourhood allocated and where can sporting facilities be found? What kind of working conditions do we find acceptable, and are the guidelines actually enforced? But it also involves decisions about what kinds of illnesses and health conditions should be researched, what types of medicine are made available or are reimbursed, what vaccination programmes there are, and who qualifies for them.

Also at the level of research on health and sickness, there are significant disparities in the scientific knowledge that exists on diseases and cures. Much more is known about certain target groups than about others. Research into symptoms and knowledge about effective treatments and medicines are primarily based on experience with certain research groups – especially white men in Western societies. Whether these insights also help in the diagnosis and treatment of other groups is unclear. We know that some ailments (for example, lactose intolerance) are more prevalent in people of Asian descent, but is this also the case for other syndromes? We now also know that observations of male patients form the basis for many standard protocols for diagnosis and treatment, which is far from optimal for other patient groups. This is certainly the case with heart attack symptoms, which are very different for women than for men and are consequently often recognized too late (see also: https://www.goredforwomen.org/).

The social gradient in health
Kate Pickett and Richard Wilkinson

Research over many decades and in many different countries has shown that people with lower socioeconomic status suffer much more ill health and have shorter life expectancy. Even within developed countries, like the United Kingdom and the Netherlands, there is an 8-10 year difference in life expectancy between neighbourhoods within the same city. That is true whether status is measured by occupational class, education, income, by whether or not you own your house, or whether you live in a richer or poorer area. In rich developed countries the scale of health disadvantage associated with being low on the social ladder varies from 2-5 years shorter life expectancy than those further up the ladder, to as much as 10, 15 or – at the extreme – as much as 20 year differences in life expectancy. Importantly, the effects are found in men and women at all ages, and for most of the main causes of death.

Typically these differences in health are not simply differences between the poor and the rest of society. Instead there is a *gradient* in health. Health gets worse at every step down the social ladder: Even the well-educated and affluent have slightly worse health than the very best educated and richest. When we have been able to take away the problem of poverty and poor health, we may thus still find that most of the pattern of health inequalities remains.

3.4

From social stigma to health

Belle Derks and Daan Scheepers

Being a member of a stigmatized or low status group has been related to a wide range of negative health outcomes. Social psychological research has identified three pathways through which these negative health outcomes emerge.

First, being the target of prejudice forms a major source of stress among people with low status. This stress has in turn been related to a range of negative health outcomes, ranging from hypertension and cardiovascular disease to type II diabetes, asthma, arthritis, osteoporosis, and Alzheimer's disease.

Second, the stress associated with low societal status also negatively affect health because of the suboptimal health behaviours it triggers. Being devalued by others can lead people to escape or avoid stress through coping strategies that directly damage their health, such as smoking, overeating, using drugs and alcohol and behaving in a risky way. At the same time, in order to refrain from eating unhealthy foods and smoking, exercise on a regular basis and adhere to medical regimes, people need to effortfully inhibit their immediate desire and replace it with behaviour that is in line with more abstract health promotion goals. Research shows that stress undermines such self-regulatory strengths thereby indirectly undermining health among the stigmatized.

A final pathway via which stigma and low societal status undermine health occurs via the suboptimal interactions between stigmatized patients and non-stigmatized healthcare providers. First, healthcare providers' prejudice towards patients with stigma can lead them to feel less empathy and provide lower quality healthcare. Moreover, interactions between the stigmatized and non-stigmatized are often awkward for both parties involved, for example due to feelings of anxiety and uncertainty. In healthcare settings, these strains can tax the executive resources of both the healthcare provider (possibly leading to suboptimal medical decisions) as well as those of the patient (reducing their ability to understand medical information).

A chain of causes

Given the political, commercial, and scientific choices that are made in this way, men and women, people from different income groups, and members of different ethnic groups face different prospects regarding their health. These differences are accumulative and can have far-reaching consequences (see Box 3.3).

In order to understand or to change the health behaviour of individuals, it is not sufficient to look at individual choices with respect to health behaviour and lifestyle, for the lifestyle choices people make and the options and constraints they face are also determined by factors on which they themselves have little influence. Moreover, certain groups in society (e.g., ethnic minorities) are also approached and treated differently due to prejudice and stigmatization – which in turn has a negative effect on their mental and physical well-being (see Box 3.4). In cases where this leads to different health outcomes, this cannot be considered an individual choice of lifestyle. Some people in society are less likely to have a long and healthy life for the simple reason that they belong to a particular group. Financial incentives are of no use here; they would only constitute punishment for circumstances that people are unable to control.

Experts agree that health differences between different groups in society arise from a chain of causes. There is ample proof that family income, the neighbourhood in which

one grows up, and the kind of work we do affect our health, regardless of the personal choices we make or the lifestyles we maintain. And yet far too little is done with these so-called 'social determinants' of health in shaping government measures to rectify the situation, because the responsibility for a healthy lifestyle is for the most part attributed to the individual. But even when government measures are applied to specific groups, they do not always have positive effects.

Separate worlds

Different groups of people often live in separate worlds. And within these groups, people influence each other in terms of how much they smoke or drink, when to go out together, whether or not to exercise together, and whether to eat traditional meals that are high in fat and low in vitamins. The fact that different groups live in separate worlds makes it more difficult to eliminate health differences. If you only have contact with people like you, you are unlikely to receive new information from them about healthy or unhealthy lifestyle habits. The most obvious solution would then seem to be to detach people as much as possible from their groups and from the environment that makes it difficult for them to act on health recommendations. But is this really the best solution?

3.5

Benefits of social inclusion

Naomi Ellemers

Different experiments show that material support, displays of solidarity, and mutual helping are more likely to occur among those who resemble each other and encounter similar life difficulties ('ingroup members'), than among those who have different life histories and backgrounds ('outgroup members'). Paradoxically, the joint experience of suffering social disadvantage, for instance due to group-based discrimination, can only intensify the realization of sharing similar fates and further cement this bond. This happens also among people who do not particularly like each other and even when they do not know each other personally. This is one explanation why people enjoy more health benefits when they live and work among those who are similar to them, even if these are materially less well off.

Further, being respected, included, and valued by others who have similar life histories and concerns is an important source of psychological resilience, that buffers people against the negative effects of stress and hardship. This is the case, even if the objective challenges they face remain the same. The awareness of being socially included and the subjective sense of group belonging enhance people's feelings of esteem and well-being. This in turn provides them with more confidence that they can effectively cope with the hardship they face. Studies systematically comparing people who feel excluded from social groups vs. socially included have demonstrated this to relate to better health outcomes over time.

The link between social support and health

Research shows that groups can also have positive effects on the health of people who belong to them. This is something that is often overlooked. The positive effects are not restricted to those groups that are relatively well off; disadvantaged groups in society can also offer their members support and thereby contribute to their well-being and health.

People prefer to have contact with people who are similar to them and who have a better understanding of what they are going through and their problems, and who give them a sense of belonging. Generally, this kind of contact with like-minded people has a positive effect on well-being. It does not matter whether the similarity involves one's position in society, one's knowledge or experience, or one's preference for certain lifestyle habits.

When people feel that they belong to a group and are appreciated by others in that group, this gives them a certain degree of psychological resilience. As a result, they experience less stress, because they know they can rely on each other for support. It gives them the confidence that they will be able to deal effectively with any problems they might run into, and it gives them the faith that others will be there to help them, which in turn ensures that they are less troubled by the difficulties they encounter (see Box 3.5).

Over the years, various studies conducted among diverse

groups of people in different countries have shown that this kind of contact is not only gratifying, but also has very positive effects on health and well-being. This 'group density effect' (see Box 3.6) applies, for instance, to elderly people who have a better social network. Other examples can be found among immigrants in the US or Europe. Living in a group with likeminded people and the social support that this provides can protect people against the negative effects of their group's adverse lifestyle or social environment. These health benefits are even visible among groups in which actual health conditions are less favourable.

The best way to reduce health disparities may therefore not be to have people detach themselves from their group to live in another environment or to change their lifestyle. If this results in them losing their social network, this may actually have negative consequences for their health. People who have more contact with other likeminded people and who are more embedded in social groups and networks also enjoy better mental and physical health. It therefore makes more sense to look at whether and how it would be possible to improve the living conditions of disadvantaged groups more generally, so that these people can support each other in developing a healthier lifestyle.

3.6

Group-density effect

Kate Pickett and Madeleine Power

Members of low status minority communities living in an area with a higher proportion of their own racial or ethnic group sometimes have better health than those who live in areas with fewer people like themselves. This is known as the 'group density' effect of neighbourhood characteristics on health.

'Group density' effects, seen in studies of mental illness and physical health, can seem counterintuitive. Usually, taking into account people's income, education and social class, living in a poorer area is associated with worse health. Members of ethnic minorities who live in areas where there are few like themselves tend to be better educated and have higher incomes than those who live in areas with a higher concentration of people of a similar ethnicity, so we would expect their health to be better. However, through the eyes of the majority community, ethnic minorities may be made more aware of belonging to a low status minority group, and experience more prejudice and discrimination. It may be that the effects of stigma offset any advantage of improved individual or neighbourhood social status, and that social support and solidarity are lost. The importance of such social factors is illustrated by the 'ethnic density' effect.

An example of this effect is shown in a study conducted in the Netherlands. Researchers found that immigrants who live in neighbourhoods where their own ethnic group was only a small proportion of the population were at increased risk for certain psychotic disorders. The risk of psychotic disorders for first and second generation immigrants from Morocco, Surinam, and Turkey was twice as high in low ethnic density neighbourhoods as in high ethnic density neighbourhoods, in which at least 65 percent of the population was immigrant.

What is fair?

The main conclusion of the research discussed in this chapter is that the causes of health disparities are not only to be found in the individual choices that people make, but that their lifestyles and health behaviours are also influenced by the groups in which they live, as well as various political choices and commercial decisions that lie beyond their control. This is because different *groups* of people face unequal health outcomes that stem from the differences in the way they are treated as a group, rather than biological or genetic differences. And although members of low-income or low-educated groups are most affected by these kinds of differences, it is debatable whether they would be better off if they were to detach themselves from their group. After all, that would mean cutting themselves loose from social support, which is precisely the factor that has a positive effect on health.

In addition, financial incentives to help people live healthier lives are not necessarily effective. As with cost-benefit analyses at the societal level, such incentives do not take into account the unequal treatment of certain groups in society. A more effective way to eradicate differences in health outcomes would be to strive for the more equitable treatment of various groups of people. This is because, more often than not, bad health is not exclusively 'one's own fault'.

4

Migration

Daan Scheepers

Migration is as old as mankind: throughout history, people have moved to areas where life is better, or at least appears to be better. Social inequality is closely linked to migration and the challenges that migration brings. The great disparity between different parts of the world is a reason for people to migrate: people will travel from areas where famine prevails to countries blessed with apparent abundance (see Figure 6).

The situation at the global level also has consequences for the societies to which migrants emigrate. Although migration can reduce inequality at a global level, it can reinforce inequality at the local level (see Box 4.1). The increase in – often cheap – labour due to the arrival of migrants affects the development of wages and the supply of jobs. Migrants need to be housed, but this means that there are fewer inexpensive housing options for others. This puts a strain on people's sense of security, in particular among those in the lower social classes. Immigration can lead to tensions, and

4.1

The birthright lottery
Joseph Heath

Every day, across the planet, more than 350,000 children are born. One of the factors that has the most significant impact on their expected quality of life –their standard of living, their health, their life expectancy– is also one of the most arbitrary. It is their country of birth, and the citizenship that they will acquire. Many have referred to this as 'the birth right lottery'. Some children win, by being born into affluent societies, while others are born into poverty. This is widely regarded as unjust. As the 'lottery' metaphor suggests, those who wind up affluent did nothing to earn that privilege, they merely got lucky. There is an important feature of the world system that significantly reinforces the effects of this lottery: The global state system permits very little migration. There is an obvious egalitarian objection to this practice. Many of the more severe inequalities between nations could be dramatically reduced if states would just open up their borders to increased migration. Within liberal states, freedom of movement is considered an important individual right. It is unclear why this right should not create a strong presumption against the forms of border control that are currently exercised internationally by states. At the same time, large-scale migration is associated with significant strains. Not least is the fact that while migration of low-skilled labour from poor countries to rich countries can reduce global inequality, it will also tend to increase domestic inequality within wealthier nations by putting downward pressure on wages. This poses a dilemma for those who are concerned about inequality. There is an impartial demand to reduce global inequality. But there is also a form of partiality involved in concern for one's co-citizens, and of the quality of civic life in one's own society. This these tensions are unequally distributed: stress and uncertainty are felt primarily by the lower socio-economic classes, while the benefits of globalization and multiculturalism are enjoyed primarily by the higher socio-economic classes. This chapter considers how social inequality influences a host society's attitude towards immigrants. We first look at the arguments currently dominating the debate on migration, before examining the added value of a moral perspective in this debate.

Figure 6
Net Migration

The current debate

The debate on migration is strongly characterized by thinking in terms of 'us and them'. Migrants are frequently referred to as 'the migrants' or 'the refugees' in both arguments for and against their admittance. Although a distinction is often made between different groups of migrants, such as refugees as opposed to so-called 'fortune-seekers', people seldom refer to migrants as unique individuals. The tendency to see migrants as a separate group makes it easier to believe that when they encounter problems, it is their own fault (see Box 4.2).

If we look at the reasoning used in the debate, economic arguments immediately stand out. An often-heard anti-immigration argument is that the arrival of migrants is bad for the economy: 'They take away our jobs'. But even those with a more positive attitude towards migrants often emphasize the added value of migrants for the economy: they are prepared to take jobs in the cleaning or crop picking sectors, which, so the argument goes, 'our own people are unwilling to do'. It is also pointed out that migrants have made the nation great over the centuries (in the case of the Netherlands, the Portuguese Jews, the Huguenots and, more recently, Surinamese footballers) and that taking a tolerant, open-minded approach has brought the nation a significant amount of economic prosperity.

partiality often takes extreme and illegitimate forms. This does nothing, however, to defeat the basic challenge, which involves articulating some form of reasonable partiality, which can be balanced against the demand to remedy the more general wrong that is the effect of the birth right lottery.

Economic reasoning does not lead to consensus

But what exactly is the scientific evidence for these instrumental arguments? Do migrants benefit the economy or do they simply cost money? A closer examination shows that the situation is more complicated than it is often believed to be. More importantly, an economic cost-benefit analysis will ultimately fail to bring consensus in the debate on immigration.

Research has shown that a rise in immigration has a slightly positive effect on economic growth. In addition, a number of myths about the economic costs of immigrants can be debunked. In general, migrants do not rely unduly on social insurance; they are primarily motivated to work. Indeed, migrants generally contribute more to social insurance than they themselves get out of it. Ironically, this is particularly the case for illegal immigrants whose employers often withhold social insurance contributions from their wages, while the illegal immigrants are themselves unable (or do not dare) to benefit from social security schemes, due to their unofficial status.

Why is the idea that immigrants are a burden on the economy so persistent, even though it is at least partly a myth? One answer lies in the belief that the economy is a *zero-sum game*: if one group gains, this means that the other group loses – and with more competitors, there is less for everyone. But a modern economy does not work in this way.

Members of the host society actually benefit from immigration – for example, because they can get ahead in their company more easily than an immigrant who doesn't speak the language very well or doesn't know the system. And the economic growth that migration generates can also have positive effects for non-immigrants. In fact, previous generations of migrants are often most at risk of being forced out of the labour market. And real problem-groups in the labour market will in any case have difficulty finding a job, even without the presence of migrants.

Although preconceptions about the economic effects of migration are often unfounded, it would be incorrect to say that immigration is automatically a driver of economic success. There are simply too many factors at play. It makes a big difference whether one looks at the short term or the long term. In the 1960s, migrant labourers were brought to the Netherlands as cheap labour. In the 1980s, however, a significant number of them became unemployed when the industries in which they worked (textiles, mining) disappeared. Another example is the current influx of refugees. In the short term, this will mostly cost money. But in the long term, refugees may bring money into the society, especially if they are highly educated (for example, in IT), quickly learn to speak the language, and integrate well into the host society in other ways. The final economic costs and benefits of migration thus depend on a number of factors.

4.2

Motivations to justify inequality

Jojanneke Van der Toorn

Although inequality, exploitation, and injustice are the order of the day, people are less likely to rebel against this than you would expect. One reason for this is that people tend to rationalize the status quo, even when the status quo puts them at a disadvantage. We simply prefer to believe that the world around us is just and that people get what they deserve because this contributes to our sense of security and control. The notion that misfortune is arbitrary is, after all, a distressing thought.

One way in which people justify the system is by using meritocratic explanations for social and economic inequality. According to this type of ideology (such as 'the American Dream'), people owe their position in society to their own efforts. This has consequences for how members of disadvantaged groups and privileged groups see themselves and others. Those who have not gotten far in life receive the blame for their own misfortunes, but we look up to those who have succeeded in life. It is for this reason that victims are often held responsible for their own adversity and success is lauded.

The tendency to believe in a just world is so strong that people sometimes accept the social order even when it works to the detriment of themselves or their group. This may seem irrational but can be explained by the fact that rationalization reduces the anxiety and insecurity that is caused by an unequal and possibly unjust world. Because of these psychological benefits, both privileged and disadvantaged groups go along with this way of thinking. For privileged groups, moreover, rationalization means that they do not have to feel guilty about retaining their privileges.

Framing the immigration debate purely in terms of economics gives rise to another problem. Research into migration trends and economic growth is mostly based on macroeconomic considerations, such as the relationship between the percentage of immigrants in a country and economic growth. However, this can lead people to forget that there are local costs associated with immigration, certainly in the short-term, such as costs related to housing, education, care, and other services. These are precisely the kinds of things that people worry about. It is primarily within the local community that people are confronted with immigrants, and for these people, the long-term benefits of accepting migrants into a country are less visible. A tension can therefore develop between macroeconomic benefits in the long term and local costs in the short term. This is something that is not sufficiently taken into account if one looks at the migration debate solely from an economic perspective.

The complexity of economic factors makes it unlikely that supporters and opponents of immigration will ever agree with each other on purely economic grounds. But there is a more fundamental reason why limiting the debate to economic issues is of little help: in forming an opinion on immigration, there are many other factors – such as identity, morality, and emotions – that play a role.

The importance of identity, morality, and emotion

Immigrant groups and the religious and cultural ideas that they bring with them can give members of the host society the feeling that their culture and identity are being eradicated. In other words, the presence of 'the other' can infringe upon their image of what makes their society distinctive. This is particularly threatening in the context of a number of other developments that put pressure on a sense of national identity. One such development is the growing individualization in society, which is already eroding the degree of cohesiveness among citizens. Another development is the increasingly abstract identities that people feel are being imposed on them (the 'European ideal'), for example as a result of globalization and the ongoing process of European integration. This combination of factors is putting pressure on people's sense of national identity. In various countries, the desire to limit immigration is motivated not solely by economic considerations, but primarily by concerns about a country's own identity (see Figure 7).

Even people who have a more positive attitude towards migrants often base their arguments on identity, however, pointing out how immigrants can enrich the sense of national identity (see Box 4.4). Part of the Canadian national identity is explicitly based on the notion that Canada is a nation of immigrants. In a similar way, the Netherlands is often presented as a country with a rich history of migration and

Figure 7

Explaining attitudes towards different groups of migrants

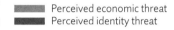

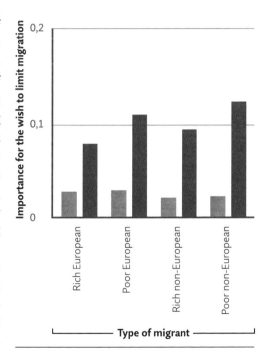

Source: Card, D., Dustmann, C. & Preston, I. (2012). 'Immigration, Wages, And Compositional Amenities'. *Journal of the European Economic Association* 10, 78-119 (table 5)

an open-minded culture and attitude to the outside world. Besides instrumental and identity-based arguments, much of the reasoning in the migration debate is moral in nature. One of the main arguments for a lenient migration policy, particularly with regard to refugees, is the moral obligation to help others in need, given that we ourselves would want to be helped under such circumstances (see Box 4.3). But the desire to limit migration is also often based on moral arguments, such as those based on a country's sovereignty and the right to defend one's own interests and to decide who may or may not enter the country (see Box 4.1).

Thus far we have talked mainly about the economic, identity-related, and moral reasoning that people use in the debate on migration. However, such arguments often ignore the fact that attitudes towards migrants are also determined by *emotions*. Many economic and identity-based arguments are eventually based on fear. Such feelings do not arise out of people contemplating the economy and national identity, but tend to be much more fundamental and nestled in the gut. People experience a feeling of menace without being able to identify what exactly they are afraid of.

'Integrated threat theory' is a socio-psychological perspective that describes three different ways in which members of other groups (such as immigrants) can be perceived as threatening. In addition to the *instrumental* (economic) and *symbolic* (identity) threat already described above, this per-

spective also identifies the feelings of fear and uncertainty that emerge during actual contact with members of other groups. This fear can be traced back to a fear of everything that is different – an emotion that is partly evolutionarily determined. This fear is particularly strong when one's own security (in particular, one's physical security) is at risk. The association of migrants with criminality and violence determines in a negative way both the quantity and the quality of contact between natives and members of migrant groups. One illustration of this is the collective fear of asylum seekers in Western European societies following the mass sexual assaults during the 2015/2016 New Year's Eve celebrations in Cologne. Fear in today's society is further reinforced by the reduced social cohesion within communities and the experience by people in multi-ethnic neighbourhoods of living alongside each other, but in separate worlds.

Social inequality colours the debate on migration
Both supporters and opponents of migration thus make use of economic, identity-based, and moral arguments. Within the host society, these arguments tend to be aligned with social class. Pro-migration positions are more often taken by those from higher social classes, whereas anti-migration views are more likely to be held by people from lower social classes. People who are less well-off have more reason to feel threatened economically, in the sense of being afraid to lose the little

they have. Also the more general uncertainty felt by those at the bottom of society makes them yearn for more stability in terms of their identity and culture. The way in which migrants threaten that culture and identity will be felt first by that part of society experiencing the highest degree of uncertainty. Members of the lower social classes come into contact more often with migrants, which is why they tend to overestimate their numbers and their influence on Dutch society. By contrast, members of the higher social classes come into contact mostly with the *idea* of migration, and not so much its direct practical consequences. And if they do come into contact with these consequences, they are more likely to be positive consequences in their case. Migrants can be cheap workers, or they might open new and interesting restaurants. Migration has positive outcomes for these people, because it confirms the identity of the Netherlands as an exemplary, tolerant country and their own personal identity as enlightened, open-minded individuals.

Local versus global identification

The instrumental, moral, and identity-based arguments that play a role in the debate on migration are often intertwined. But the different viewpoints they advocate are usually rooted in different levels of identification, namely, a more *local* versus a broader, more *global* identification. The argument that we are morally obliged to help someone in need, re-

4.3

Inequality, migration and moral duties

Pauline Kleingeld

The severe global inequality in standards of living gives people living in poverty reason to migrate to provide for their families or improve their own lives. States that are better off, in the sense that they are relatively affluent, have a duty, defined by international law, to admit refugees. But they do not have a similar duty to admit people who are fleeing poverty. Do citizens of affluent states have a moral duty to support opening the borders to immigrants?

This question is often answered negatively, on the grounds that states and their populations have a legitimate interest in preserving their culture, institutions, standard of living, and other achievements that might be threatened by mass immigration. However, even in cases in which these threats are real and restrictions on immigration legitimate, such states still have a moral duty to alleviate unjust inequalities.

First, insofar as the poverty of others elsewhere is the result of an unjust global economic system that benefits the affluent, the affluent have a duty to promote a more just system, rather than continuing to profit from injustice. They could do so, for example, through political activity or their consumer behaviour. Second, it is widely acknowledged that the affluent have a general moral duty to assist others in need, meaning that they have a duty to assist people suffering from poverty elsewhere in the world. Such assistance may range from influencing political institutions to promoting the improvement of education systems; obviously, what constitutes the best way depends on the specific causes of poverty and the most effective ways to alleviate it.

gardless of his or her origin, is based on a global, universal identification with 'mankind'. The equally moral argument that it is someone's right to defend the interests of his or her village or country is, on the other hand, based on a more local identification with one's own community. In our discussion of the economic factors, we already touched upon the fact that pro-migration arguments are usually based on macroeconomic theories that have been developed by policymakers, while anti-immigration arguments often stem from threats to jobs and security at the local level. The anti-immigration arguments are usually based more on a local identification, and the pro-immigration arguments on a global identification.

This distinction between local and global levels of identification can be found in various theories and observations. The sociologist Abram de Swaan, for example, has shown how 'expanding circles of identification' have emerged in the course of evolution. While identification with one's own family is as old as mankind, it was not until the hunter-gatherer period that identification with a wider community (tribe, village, region) emerged. More recently, a new kind of identification has emerged – identification with more abstract categories based on ethnicity, the nation-state, and even mankind in general.

As indicated above, socio-cultural factors and different interests allow higher social classes to identify more easily

with the global level, while the local level of identification is more important for the lower social classes. But there are also more fundamental psychological reasons for this difference in identification. People who have more status and power are more inclined to perceive the world at a more global and abstract level ('the big picture'), while people and groups with less status and power are more inclined to view the world at a more concrete level ('the details'). If you are able to operate relatively independently of others, you can afford to pay attention to the big picture and to identify the opportunities. But if you are heavily dependent on others for even your most basic needs, you become more focused on your surroundings and the constraints that you face. Research has shown, for example, that experiencing a lack of control over one's situation invokes feelings of threat and focuses one's attention on the details of the local situation, while those who have more opportunities to turn a situation to their own advantage tend to see things as positive challenges, are more focused on the big picture, and can perceive broader horizons. The German Chancellor Angela Merkel used the motto 'Wir schaffen das!' ('we will do it!') to present the immigration problem as a positive challenge. But given the fundamental psychological processes described above, it was to be expected that her appeal would fall on deaf ears among members of the lower social classes.

A step forward in the debate on immigration

Does it help to take account of the fact that the arguments in the debate on immigration are partly rooted in different levels of identification that have come about as a result of social inequality? In any case, acknowledging this does make clear that we need to find a balance between the interests of one's own group on the one hand, and on the other hand, universal and thus transnational human rights (see Box 4.3). In philosophy, such a balance is called 'reasonable partiality' (see Box 4.1). One of the ways this could take shape is by deploying a dual identification that allows people to identify simultaneously with both the local and the global communities.

Within philosophy, the idea of simultaneous identification with a local group (community, village) and the global group ('mankind') goes back to the Stoics and their cosmopolitan ideal. When Diogenes was asked where he came from, he answered: 'I am a citizen of the World'. In the Stoic view of morality, world citizenship was the way to fulfil one's moral duty to treat everyone as equals. Later Stoic views on cosmopolitanism nuanced this radical view somewhat in the sense that everyone belongs to two communities: the local community in which one is born and the world community. According to this more moderate view of cosmopolitanism, these two loyalties are not in conflict with each other, be-

cause world citizenship is compatible with local forms of political organization.

How does one embody this ideal in practice? In psychology, the idea of a dual identity has mainly been applied to optimize relationships in a multicultural society. For example, it turns out that one can feel both 'Moroccan' and 'Dutch' at the same time. The simultaneous identification with one's own sub-group and with an overarching category is an effective way of bringing groups together. This was made evident in research on successful and less successful mergers of companies. A dual identity is useful because it allows the higher-level category to bind together the members of the different groups, while at the same time retaining each person's bond with their own sub-group and that sub-group's own character: in other words, unity in diversity.

Shifting identities

Repeating anti- and pro-immigration standpoints will not bring us any further in the public debate on migration. For a genuine dialogue that leads to practicable solutions, these two camps must first be brought closer together. To achieve this, those who are opposed to immigration should be reminded of the moral arguments that would help them to identify with a more global level. Those who are in favour of migration could take greater account of the instrumental considerations that play a role if they are to identify with the local level as well. This would deepen the pro-immigration camp's understanding of the problems that arise from inequality at the local level, while the anti-immigration camp would gain more insight into the problems arising from global inequality and the opportunities that migration can offer. The foundation for such shifts in identification is certainly there (see Box 4.4).

Concerns about immigration are not only based on cold economic calculations, but precisely on empathy with 'our own people' within the local community, in particular the more vulnerable among them, such as the elderly and those living on or under the minimum wage. People who get to know immigrants, their families, and the problems they encounter will be quicker to see them as vulnerable members of the local community, instead of as intruders. Many of the initiatives currently being taken for the reception of asylum seekers are local in nature. In addition, there are plenty of examples of entire village communities coming to the defence of asylum seekers (and their children) who have exhausted all legal processes and are facing deportation. This is precisely what philosopher Martha Nussbaum means when she refers to 'pulling the outer circles inside': abstract ideas about a world community and universal equality become concrete when people can relate them to what they actually see happening in their own community.

4.4

Social identities

Naomi Ellemers

Humans are social beings. In addition to the unique characteristics that define their personal identities, people can think of themselves and others as members of social groups. The groups that we belong to – and the features that characterize these groups – provide us with a sense of who we are, where we belong, and how we are similar to some individuals and distinct from others. Such social identities can be defined very concretely (I am a Londoner) or at a higher level of abstraction (I am a human being). Being included, respected and valued by others who acknowledge who we are and what we stand for is very important. This group-based sense of self – which is referred to as our 'social identity' – also functions as an important guideline for individual behavioural choices. Norms and practices that characterize the groups we belong to ('ingroup' norms) have a greater impact on our behaviour than those that stem from groups we see as less relevant to the self ('outgroups'), even if the behaviours they prescribe and the individual gains that can be achieved by behaving in this way are identical.

One illustration of a leader who made this shift is Barack Obama. In his 2008 speech entitled 'A more perfect union', he spoke out, for the first time as a presidential candidate, about racial problems in his country. He delved into the anger felt by many black citizens about the social inequality that had formed over the centuries. But he also spoke about the roots of racism among white citizens from the lower socio-economic classes and the (legitimate) anger they felt about their position and their opportunities. According to Obama, these people had just as little reason to feel privileged by their ethnicity. Without legitimizing racism as the outcome, he shifted his analysis from an abstract, moral level to the grassroots level in which racism is rooted. He did not refer to abstract, moral principles ('thou shalt not discriminate!'), but instead showed sensitivity to the legitimate, everyday concerns of regular citizens from the lower socio-economic classes. Some analysts believe that it was this speech that brought him victory in the elections later that year.

5

Climate change

Belle Derks

When we think of the issues surrounding climate change, its association with social inequality is not immediately clear. Climate change is a worldwide problem – the world is warming up, the world's glaciers are melting – and this is something we need to solve in a practical way. But what does this have to do with social inequality? In this chapter, we will show that social inequality is closely intertwined with climate change. We live in a world full of differences, including when it comes to climate change: there is disparity in who will experience the most negative consequences of climate change (the poor countries and future generations), but also in who emits the most CO_2 (see Figure 8), who has the most options when it comes to doing something about climate change, and who can most easily dodge their responsibilities (the richer countries; see Box 5.1). These different forms of social inequality imply that there is a moral dimension to the climate debate. As in the previous chapters, we will argue that this moral dimension is often sidestepped

Figure 8
Inequality in climate change

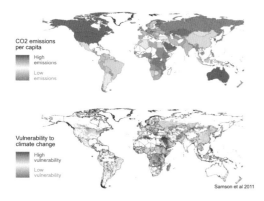

CO2 emissions per capita
- High emissions
- Low emissions

Vulnerability to climate change
- High vulnerability
- Low vulnerability

Samson et al 2011

Top: CO₂ emissions per person
Bottom: Vulnerability to climate change impact

Source: http://www.skepticalscience.com/graphics.php?g=15

in favour of a more economic and instrumental approach to environmental issues. This is unfortunate, because it is precisely the moral approach to climate change that provides promising opportunities for tackling this issue together.

Climate change: the perfect moral storm
Why is it so difficult to convince people, companies, and governments that we need to act together *now* if we want to curb climate change? The philosopher Stephen Gardiner suggests that the problem of climate change has a few peculiar characteristics that make it difficult for people to take the necessary steps to solve it. He calls it the 'perfect moral storm', using the analogy of a rare combination of weather circumstances referred to as 'the perfect storm'. While each of the factors that influence the climate itself constitutes a serious constraint on our ability to take decisions, when they occur simultaneously, they create the perfect moral storm. In this storm, people, companies, and governments doubt *whether* they should take action to stop climate change and *what* that action should be. More specifically, this perfect moral storm is shaped by a combination of three storms: a 'world storm', a 'temporal storm', and a 'theoretical storm'.

First, we have the *world storm*. Climate change is a problem that can only be solved through global cooperation. Greenhouse gases that are emitted in one place have an effect on the rest of the world. Our environmentally friendly behaviour can be offset by CO_2 emissions in other countries. Behavioural economists see the climate issue as a *social dilemma*, a situation in which people must choose between their own interests and the interests of the community. The world as a whole benefits if every individual and each country reduces its use of fossil fuels, but individual people and countries benefit the most if others reduce their emissions while they themselves continue unabated in their consumption and production.

There is, moreover, great disparity *between* countries: while poor countries suffer more from climate change due to their geographical location (think of droughts and flooding), the responsibility for climate change lies primarily with the richer Western countries that generated the most emissions in the past. But the world lacks a well-functioning system of global governance. The poorer countries are in no position to force the richer countries to assume their responsibility, while the richer countries have enough political power to choose not to participate in climate treaties. All these factors diminish the likelihood of finding a good, collective solution to the issue of climate change.

Second, there is the *temporal storm:* climate change is a problem postponed. The climate reacts very slowly, which means that our behaviour will have disastrous consequences only in the distant future. Moreover, reducing the use of fossil fuels entails high costs for the current generation

(for example, less economic growth and consumption), but mostly positive effects in the future (after 2050). Future generations have no voice in the debate on climate change, and their interests are not well represented. Psychological research shows that most people already find it difficult to postpone rewards for themselves, so you can imagine how difficult people find it to do something now to reward the next generation. National governments have a short lifespan and are primarily focused on maximizing outcomes for their current voters instead of outcomes for future generations. This is known as 'contempocentrism'. There is a great temptation to pass the buck to the next generation. At the same time, scientists warn that if we wait to take action, future generations will have to employ much more drastic measures to turn the tide than those we would have to employ now to achieve the same result.

And finally, a *theoretical storm* is raging. We humans lack the intellectual tools truly to understand and tackle the magnitude of the climate problem. Scientists assume that a rational analysis of the climate issue is *the* way to achieve a solution. For example, they approach the debate on climate change from a technical perspective ('How do we reduce CO_2 emissions?', 'How can we take greenhouse gases out of the atmosphere?') or an economic perspective ('How heavily should the benefits for future generations weigh in our current choices?'). Most theoretical approaches also assume that individuals and countries can be convinced to act in a rational way to solve this collective problem. But all these approaches ignore the magnitude and complexity of the climate issue and the inability of humankind to understand or solve a problem of this type. At the same time, debates on climate change give people an excuse not to act or to blame somebody else. They can also make people unrealistically confident that scientists will find a solution to the climate problem (described as the *technological fix*) or can even lead to denial that it is a problem ('Even the scientists can't agree on it!'). If we wait to take action until it is crystal clear what we should do about climate change, it will be too late.

The combination of the peculiar characteristics of the climate problem (the world, temporal, and theoretical storms) creates a superstorm that contributes to a new problem, namely that of *moral corruption*. The problem of climate change is so big and so complex that it makes it easy for us to postpone action. It is easy to do nothing based on the argument that we don't know enough yet about climate change to decide how we are going to solve it. By addressing only a part of the problem while ignoring other aspects, we can easily convey the impression that we are doing our best to stop climate change. While climate conferences are being convened to try to allocate responsibility for a global problem, they can have the effect of making us feel good about climate treaties that will have only limited positive effects on future generations. The perfect moral storm created by climate change makes it easy for the current generation to go on behaving in a manner that will damage future generations without having to feel bad about it.

Instrumental solutions to the climate problem

Many climate scientists agree that in order to stop climate change, governments must take drastic collective action as soon as possible. At the same time, economists emphasize that such measures would bring high costs and that over-ambitious measures would unnecessarily damage the economies of individual countries. Citizens and governments are dependent on each other to solve the climate problem. But acting in the collective interest by reducing our dependency on fossil fuels also brings high costs, such as the costs involved in investing in new climate-neutral technologies and the income that a country might forgo if the production and export of goods declines. These high costs of cooperation make it tempting for individual countries to not cooperate and to let the problem be solved by other countries.

When the climate problem is seen as a social dilemma, then the logical solution is to arrive at an even distribution of the costs through international treaties. One example of this is the Kyoto Protocol, a treaty signed by a large number of industrialized countries in which the rights to emit greenhouse gases and the obligations to reduce emissions are

Climate justice
Neelke Doorn

Emissions, wastes, and resource depletion all pose threats to living organisms, including human beings. Because environmental risks do not necessarily materialize at the place where they originate from, the risks and benefits associated with environmental impact are not equally distributed.

On a local scale, those living in high-poverty and ethnic minority groups are the ones often suffering most from these environmental risks. They live closest to smoke emitting factories, polluting highways or waste disposals. These groups are often disadvantaged on several other aspects as well, like having poor labour conditions, low levels of education, and low levels of political participation.

On a global scale, the unequal distribution of environmental risks and benefits associated with these risks is equally pressing. The countries that contribute most to climate change are not the ones that suffer the gravest impact. The average per capita CO_2 emission in the US, for example, is about 16.5 ton and that of the European Union is 6.7 ton. But a country like Bangladesh, that is extremely vulnerable to climate change due to the increased risk of flooding, has a per capita CO_2 emission of only 0.4 ton.

The term *climate justice* is often used to refer to these global inequalities and the responsibility to take action to reduce climate change. There are two main arguments that point at affluent countries having a responsibility in this regard. First, as mentioned above, the causal contribution to climate change by affluent countries is much larger than that of poorer countries. Second, affluent countries are generally better able to take action to reduce climate change.

distributed. Although these climate treaties can be a good first step in the direction of a reduction of CO_2 emissions, they do have disadvantages. An economic approach to the climate problem calls for setting a price for pollution and allowing the market to do its job. The idea is that if the price is high enough, companies will of their own accord emit fewer greenhouse gases.

But research shows that trade in emissions does not lead to a reduction of CO_2 emissions because it may reduce investments in emission-reducing technologies that would actually reduce climate change (see Box 5.2). The Kyoto Protocol and the emissions trading system of the European Union have not led to any form of reduction in emissions to date. The trade in emissions creates a short-term focus on economic costs and benefits and a diffusion of responsibility, instead of the long-term vision necessary to reduce CO_2 emissions. Such a trading system only leads to a reduction in greenhouse gas emissions when the maximum allowable emission is low. But when establishing the current system, a surplus of emissions rights was distributed. As a result, the price is very low, making it cheaper for companies to buy additional emissions rights than to invest in technology that limits these emissions. In addition, many companies currently have a surplus of emissions rights due to the effects of the economic crisis (as a result of the decline in production). Economic approaches to the climate problem *seem* simple

5.2

Drawbacks of carbon emission rights trading

Servaas Storm

The rationale for carbon trading is that a steady pressure from a high carbon price, which internalizes carbon's external cost, will motivate firms and individuals to reduce their carbon emissions now and invest in efficient carbon-avoiding alternative technologies to reduce emissions in the future. But can a 'corrective' price for carbon bring about the radical de-carbonization of our energy, transportation, production and consumption systems, necessary for a zero-carbon society? The answer is: No.

For a start, setting the *right* 'corrective' price for carbon is impossible because carbon's external cost (which depends on the future impacts of warming) is unknown. Second, climate stabilization requires a fundamental 'disruption' of hydrocarbon energy infrastructures, and a massive upsetting of vested interests in the fossil-fuel economy. If the carbon price is to incentivize firms to bring about this radical change, it has to be high enough to help private firms recover their investment costs plus a substantial premium for market risks associated with deploying risky, unproven technologies. Imperfect real-life carbon markets are unlikely to produce such a high price, but will instead exhibit disproportionate price instability. Worse, carbon trading may encourage the industries most addicted to fossil fuels to carry on much as before, because it is less costly for them to purchase carbon credits from others than switch to renewable energy.

Finally, carbon pricing raises serious distributive concerns. The reason is that to avoid 'carbon leakage', the carbon price must be the same for everyone everywhere. A high enough global carbon price will considerably raise energy prices – one study predicts that the price of 1 litre of gasoline will increase by 1 US$ – and the effect of this on the world's three billion poor, who have to survive on less than 2,5 US$ per person per day, would be devastating.

and rational, but there are also drawbacks, because they can lead to greater social inequality in the world. Take, for example, the recent growth in the use of biofuels. The use of biofuels in our part of the world leads to food crises and an increase in food prices in other parts of the world, because land and crops that had otherwise been used for food production are now being used to produce our 'sustainable' fuel. Similarly, there are disadvantages to emissions trading and a high price for fossil fuels, because they enable richer countries to buy emissions allowances from poorer countries, which in turn is likely to hinder production and economic growth in poorer parts of the world.

Also with regard to the intergenerational aspect of climate change – the fact that future generations will suffer more from climate change and are dependent on the choices we make now – there are drawbacks to a purely economic approach. When you develop an economic model comparing the financial costs and the environmental benefits, then you must weigh the costs of climate measures for the present generation against the benefits for future generations. It is debatable whether these are economic considerations or whether they are in fact moral considerations. If you were only concerned with economic outcomes, then the balance would quickly come out in favour of the current generation. And this is also the most commonly heard criticism of cost-benefit analyses in the context of climate change. In many of these models, the financial costs of a climate-neutral economy are given too much weight, and they do not take sufficient account of the possible catastrophic consequences of our current behaviour in the future, because these effects are still uncertain. These model-based approaches cannot cope with uncertainty and thus will not stimulate the policy turnaround that is needed to stop climate change.

At the level of the individual, environmentally-friendly behaviour on the part of consumers can be seen as a dilemma between self-interest (consume as much as you want) and the interest of the community (tackling climate change). One instrumental approach to this dilemma would be for governments to encourage environmentally-friendly behaviour by reducing the costs that such behaviour entails. We could reward such behaviour with financial incentives such as subsidies for solar panels and tax benefits for hybrid cars, or information highlighting the financial benefits of saving energy. But psychological research shows that these economic approaches have a limited positive impact on consumers. Insofar as financial incentives encourage environmentally-friendly behaviour, this behaviour often disappears quickly once the financial incentive is removed. Moreover, it turns out that the emphasis on the financial aspects of decisions displaces other motives that people might have for behaving in an environmentally-friendly

5.3

Carbon responsibility

Servaas Storm

The world's countries contribute different amounts of heat-trapping gasses to the atmosphere. The six biggest carbon emitters – China, the U.S.A., the E.U., India, Russia and Japan – account for almost 70% of annual global greenhouse gas (GHG) emissions. Heavily reliant on fossil fuels for electricity and steel production, China emits nearly twice the amount of GHG as the U.S. and while the production-based carbon intensity of China's economy is on a rising trend, carbon intensities of the U.S. and the European economies have been declining for two decades. Hence, it is argued that China, and the other 'emerging economies', will determine the fate of global warming, as they are 'responsible' for most of current and future GHG emission growth.

There is more to this picture than meets the eye, however. Over the past 25 years, the U.S. and the E.U. have relocated or outsourced much of their carbon-intensive (manufacturing) activities to newly industrializing countries including China. The rich OECD countries have become *net carbon importers* (importing emissions embodied in the manufactured goods 'made in China'). This means that part of the (rising) carbon emissions in China and other emerging economies arise in the production of goods, exported to and consumed by the U.S. and E.U. Empirical evidence on consumption-based CO_2 emissions (which include all carbon emissions associated with consumption, production and transportation of commodities along internationally fragmented global commodity chains) shows that carbon intensities of U.S. and E.U. *consumption* has been steadily increasing until now. Carbon responsibility is different when defined in terms of consumption.

manner. Suppose you are about to buy a new car, and you are considering buying a fuel-efficient car because you think it is important to do your bit for the environment. It turns out that the government has introduced various tax breaks for buying a hybrid car. You end up buying an energy-efficient car, but you're no longer sure whether you did so because you believe in the importance of environmentally-friendly behaviour (an intrinsic motivation) or because of the financial benefits (an extrinsic motivation). Chances are that this experience will undermine future environmental behaviour, because your intrinsic motivation has been partly transformed into an extrinsic motivation. The greater the extrinsic reasons for buying a hybrid car – tax benefits as opposed to environmental considerations – the less you will be inclined to take the trouble to run the car on electricity instead of gasoline. And when all of the financial incentives for buying an environmentally-friendly car have disappeared (which is a real prospect, given the variability of government policy), it is likely that economic considerations will supersede environmental considerations, meaning that people choose cheap instead of fuel-efficient cars.

Economic and instrumental solutions to climate change thus have their limitations. How, then, could a moral perspective contribute to solving this problem?

Moral dimensions of the climate issue

As with the other three social themes in this book, scientists involved in the climate debate are also increasingly beginning to stress the importance of moral considerations in the search for solutions. Several philosophers and economists have pointed out the limitations of instrumental approaches in solving the climate problem. Their main argument is that we can no longer walk away from our responsibility towards future generations and social inequality in the world. And economic approaches do not really lead to a collective solution that works for poor countries and for future generations. A uniform distribution across countries of the costs of solving the problem of climate change would lead to greater social inequality and is therefore untenable. A tax on greenhouse gas emissions could easily be borne by richer countries, but would hold back the economic development of poorer countries. Moreover, whereas rich Western countries such as the US and Western European countries appear to be reducing their emissions, they are in fact outsourcing their production to countries with growing economies (such as China and India) while their own consumption only continues to grow (see Box 5.3). Thus, although one collective solution might appear to be the allocation of environmental measures, in practice this is not the case. In the transition to a climate-neutral world, we must not think in terms of a uniform distribution, but rather in terms of a fair distribution of the costs.

More and more scientists are beginning to contend that if we want to reach a workable collective solution to environmental issues, we need to take a moral approach. One example of such an ethical approach is the *Greenhouse Developments Rights Framework* proposed by various environmental economists. The bottom line of this proposal is that the world's poor should be exempted from the costs entailed in solving the climate problem. The framework is premised on notions of responsibility and capability, both of which are determined on the basis of a threshold level of development. People who live below this threshold should be allowed to focus mainly on surviving and developing, for they bear little historical responsibility for climate change and should not have to bear the burden of solving this problem. The responsibility must be borne by the people with incomes above the threshold, regardless of the country in which they live. This approach leads to a completely different distribution of the costs of climate change – a division in which richer countries that currently emit fewer greenhouse gases than emerging economies such as China and India *are* held responsible for solving the climate problem.

The intergenerational aspect of climate change also compels us to take a moral approach. For the present generation, it is very advantageous and easy to pass on to the next generation the responsibility for solving the problems that

5.4

Environmental justice, emotions and motivation

Sabine Roeser

Few people are willing to significantly adapt their lifestyle in order to reduce their ecological footprint. Several scholars have proposed that the missing link in communication about climate change is the role of emotions in enticing a lifestyle that diminishes climate change. Emotions may affect people's environmental behaviour in two ways: They lead to greater awareness of the problems, and they increase people's motivation to do something about climate change. Yet, emotions are generally excluded from communication and political decision-making about risky technologies and climate change, because of the assumption that emotions are irrational and misleading.

However, this assumption is based on a narrow understanding of emotions that is challenged by insights from emotion researchers who emphasize that emotions can be an important source of practical rationality and moral insight. Quantitative approaches to risk only look at net outcomes at a high level of aggregation; they do not look into other ethical issues such as justice, fairness, autonomy and equality. In my research I argue that emotions such as sympathy, compassion, indignation, and feelings of responsibility can more strongly draw our attention to such moral values. For example, by providing people with concrete narratives of those who undergo the effects of climate change, distant others who can otherwise easily be neglected come uncomfortably close, which can elicit compassion, and force people to critically assess their own behaviour. Furthermore, the experience of moral emotions more strongly enhances people's motivation to act than purely rational, abstract knowledge about climate change, even if it means that we have to make personal sacrifices, such as adjusting our lifestyle. Communication about climate change should appeal to reflective moral emotions such as sympathy and compassion, as these can give rise to critical ethical reflection and motivate us to act in a sustainable way.

climate change will cause. Moreover, the temporal nature of our current institutions (governance at the national and international levels) and their focus on the present generation make them ill-equipped to deal with climate change. While an economic approach to the problem automatically emphasizes the high costs and low benefits for the current generation, a moral approach can lead to a long-term perspective and a sense of responsibility for the future. One proposal, by the above-mentioned philosopher Gardiner, calls for the establishment of a global constitutional institution that would function as the voice of future generations. This constitutional institution must explicitly address the impact of current policies on future generations in order to minimize the effect of moral corruption in the decisions taken by the current generation.

In the field of psychology as well, a number of studies on environmental behaviour show that morality rather than financial gain can be a powerful incentive for environmentally-friendly behaviour. Environmental campaigns that promote energy savings (for example, using less fuel by making sure your tires are properly inflated) appear to have more influence on behaviour when they emphasize a moral motive ('protect the environment') than when they emphasize a financial motive ('save money'). As we have seen in earlier chapters, the underlying reason is that people consider it very important to be moral individuals, as a result of which they are more motivated to engage in behaviour that stresses their morality than behaviour that results in financial gain. Indeed, the emotions that are evoked when we think about morality, such as compassion and indignation, turn out to be strong predictors of motivation (see Box 5.4).

Another way to highlight the importance of morality and thereby to motivate environmental behaviour is to encourage people to think about their legacy and how they want to be remembered by others. This ensures that long-term goals are given more priority and that concern for others in the future (such as children and grandchildren) becomes an important motive behind people's choices. Research shows that people who think about their legacy donate more money to charities dedicated to the environment, are more motivated to combat climate change, and also come to believe more strongly that climate change is a reality that needs to be addressed.

And finally, from a global perspective, it turns out that morality motivates people to stand behind ambitious environmental policies. A worldwide study has shown that people consider it more important to do something about climate change once they realize that not only is this kind of policy good for the environment, but that it also says something about the society in which we live. If people realize that a society that cares about the environment is a society that has more morally upright and engaged people, they will also be more supportive of measures to protect the environment.

Conclusion

To confront the climate problem, the current generation of world citizens must take action quickly as a collective to curb the use of fossil fuels. Although economic approaches to encourage environmentally-friendly behaviour such as cost-benefit analyses, emissions trading systems, and financial incentives *appear* to be effective approaches, they divert us from the scale and magnitude of the problem and only motivate people and politicians to think about achieving the greatest gains, rather than taking collective responsibility. A moral approach to the climate problem would lead to more effective solutions, because it would motivate people and countries to look for *real* solutions that would actually mitigate the climate problem and the social inequality that results from it.

References and further reading

Chapter 1: Social inequality: Myths and facts

Bandura, A. (2016). *Moral Disengagement: How People Do Harm and Live With Themselves*. New York: Worth Publishers.

Blom, F., Steffens, T., Brekelmans, R. & Boschloo, M. (2016). *Inclusiveness in Everyone's Best Interest: A Priority for Politics and Business*. Boston: Boston Consulting Group.

Cudd, A. E. (2006). *Analyzing Oppression*. New York, NY: Oxford University Press.
This book argues that rational choices of oppressed individuals contribute to their own oppression. The oppressed come to believe that they suffer personal failings and this belief appears to absolve society from responsibility.

Costanza, R., Kubiszewski, I., Giovannini, E., Lovins, H., McGlade, J., Pickett, K.W. et al. & Wilkinson, R. (2014). 'Development: Time to Dethrone GDP'. *Nature* 505, 282-285.

DiTomaso, N. (2013). *The American Non-Dilemma: Racial Inequality Without Racism*. New York, NY: Russell Sage Foundation.
Explains how racial inequality is reproduced because people differ in the opportunities they receive.

Does, S., Derks, B. & Ellemers, N. (2011). 'Thou shall not discriminate: How emphasizing moral ideals rather than obligations increases whites' support for social equality'. *Journal of Experimental Social Psychology* 47, 562-571.

Ellemers, N. (2012). 'The Group Self'. *Science* 336, 848-852.
Reviews evidence showing when and why people think, feel, and act as group members instead of as separate individuals, and explains how this relates to social inequality.

Heath, J. (2015). *Morality, Competition and the Firm*. Oxford: Oxford University Press.
The most influential argument for equality as a principle of justice invokes the idea of a social contract. This article explores some of the difficulties associated with a contractualist view.

Heath, J. (2010). *Economics Without Illusions: Debunking the Myths of Modern Capitalism*. New York, NY: Crown Publishing Group.

Heath, J. (2008). 'Political Egalitarianism'. *Social Theory and Practice* 34, 485-516.
It is a standard view among philosophers that a theory of justice for a liberal society will need to be 'political', in the sense that it must be presuppose the correctness of any of the more specific moral and religious views that are present, but not universally shared, in the population. This article examines the question of how a commitment to equality would need to be formulated, in order to 'political' in this sense of the term.

Hindriks, F. (2014). 'How autonomous are collective agents? Corporate rights and normative individualism'. *Erkenntnis* 79 (S9), 1565-1585.
This book maintains that organizations can plausibly be regarded as moral agents that can be held morally responsible.

Hindriks, F. (2015). 'How does reasoning (fail to) contribute to moral judgment? Dumbfounding and disengagement'. *Ethical Theory and Moral Practice* 18, 237-250.
Moral reasoning is presented as a cognitive process that is triggered by emotions including feelings of anticipatory guilt, guilt that often precedes the performance of a harmful action.

Hirsch, F. (2005). *Social Limits to Growth.* London: Routledge.
   In this classic work, Hirsch argues that as societies become wealthier, the differences in material possessions between income classes become less significant, it is the social qualities of the goods that remain the major point of differentiation. As a result, the amount of increased happiness obtainable through further growth declines, while the benefits of redistribution and greater equality, increase.

Kubiszewski, I., Costanza, R., Franco, C., Lawn, P., Talberth, J., Jackson, T. et al. (2013). 'Beyond GDP: Measuring and achieving global genuine progress'. *Ecological Economics* 93, 57-68.
   Global Gross Domestic Product (GDP) has increased more than three-fold since 1950 but sustainable wellbeing, estimated by the Genuine Progress Indicator (GPI), has decreased since 1978. This study looks at 17 countries over 50 years and concludes that if income were distributed more equitably around the globe, the current world GDP could support almost 10 billion people at $7000/capita.

Nussbaum, M.C. (2000). *Women and Human Development.* Cambridge: Cambridge University Press.
   Nussbaum argues that international political and economic thought should be aware of gender difference as a problem of justice that also explain problems of women in developing countries.

Peil, J. & Van Staveren, I. (eds.) (2009). *Handbook of Economics and Ethics.* Cheltenham: Edward Elgar.

Piketty, T. (2014). *Capital in the 21st Century.* Cambridge: Harvard University Press.
   One of the major changes in the sources of material inequality in the 20th century was a shift away from inheritance toward income as a major source of inequality. Piketty argues that this is a temporary phenomenon, and that as the return on capital continues to outstrip the general rate of growth in the economy, there will be a reversion to inherited wealth as a major source of material inequality.

Power, M. & Stacey. T. (2014). Course correction. London: The Equality Trust.
   This report explores the relationship between top personal income tax rates, economic growth, and economic inequality. It argues that a higher top rate of income tax could reduce high pay and, in doing so, deliver wider economic and social benefits.

Rawls, J. (1971). *A Theory of Justice.* Boston, MA: Harvard University Press.
   In this seminal book philosopher John Rawls develops a theory of justice as fairness. With his thought experiment of imagining ourselves behind a veil of ignorance where we do not know our own socio-economic situation, he argues that reasonably we should endorse policies that maximize the well-being of those who are worst off in society.

Shachar, A. (2009). *The Birthright Lottery: Citizenship and Global Inequality.* Cambridge: Harvard University Press.
   This book introduces the analogy between 'being born in a rich country' and 'having won the lottery'. Shachar argues that the right to citizenship should be treated as a type of property, handed down from one generation to the next. Global inequality could then be addressed by levying a tax on those who have inherited the more valuable forms of property.

Scheepers D. & Ellemers N. (2005). 'When the pressure is up: The assessment of social identity threat in low and high status groups'. *Journal of Experimental Social Psychology* 41, 192-200.

Sen, A. (2009). *The Idea of Justice.* Cambridge: Allen Lane & Harvard University Press.
   In this book, Amartya Sen contrasts his own theory of justice with so-called ideal theories of justice. Sen argues that, even if we lack a fully established abstract ideal of justice, we can still evaluate the fairness of different institutions. Outcomes are considered just to the degree that they contribute to individual people's capabilities. This book provides a clear and accessible introduction to Sen's capabilities approach, which is used by, amongst other, the United Nations for policy evaluations.

Stiglitz, J.E. (2012). *The Price of Inequality: How Today's Divided Society Endangers Our Future*. New York, NY: W.W. Norton & Company.
> Stiglitz focuses on runaway income growth among the top 1%, arguing that it is a consequence of market failure in the financial sector, and as well as in firm governance. He emphasizes that this is a consequence, not of the ordinary operations of markets, but of the failure of markets to control rent-seeking. He analyses the negative consequences of this growing inequality, especially for the quality of democratic decision-making in the United States.

Uslaner, E. (2002). *The Moral Foundations of Trust*. Cambridge: Cambridge University Press.
> Explains why people trust others and why it matters, showing that trusting people are more likely to give through charity and volunteering and trusting societies are more likely to redistribute resources from the rich to the poor. Traces the decline in trust in the United States in relation to declining optimism and increasing economic inequality.

Van Bavel, B. (2016). *The Invisible Hand? How Market Economies Have Emerged and Declined Since AD 500*. Oxford: Oxford University Press.
> This book challenges our confidence in free market economies as the best way to predict and influence human behaviour. A historical analysis going back to AD 500 shows that there hasn't been a single market economy hat survived in the long run.

Van Nunspeet, F., Ellemers, N. & Derks, B. (2015). 'Reducing implicit bias: How moral motivation helps people refrain from making 'automatic' prejudiced associations'. *Translational Issues in Psychological Science* 1, 382-391.

Young, I. (2011). *Responsibility for Justice*. Oxford: Oxford University Press.
> This book argues against considering justice as a matter of personal responsibility and instead argues in favour of collective responsibility.

Wilkinson R. & Pickett K. (2014). 'The world we need'. *International Journal of Labour Research* 6, 17-34.

Zsolnai, L. (2016). '*Moral Disengagement: How People Do Harm and Live With Themselves*, by Albert Bandura. New York, NY: Macmillan, 2016. 544 pp. ISBN: 978-1-4641-6005-9'. *Business Ethics Quarterly* 26, 426-429.

Chapter 2: Education and work

Arrow, K.J., Bowles, S. & Durlauf, S.N. (2000). *Meritocracy and Economic Inequality*. Princeton, NJ: Princeton University Press.
> This volume of essays discusses how inequality of opportunity contributes to economic inequality and what can be done to counteract this.

Dovidio, J.F., Hewstone, M., Glick, P. & Esses, V. (eds.) (2010). *Handbook of Prejudice, Stereotyping, and Discrimination*. London: Sage.

Eagly, A.H. & Carli, L.L. (2008). *Through the Labyrinth: The Truth about How Women Become Leaders*. Boston, MA: Harvard Business School Press.
> This book discusses the barriers that women face on their way to the top due to the fact that leadership has so long been associated with men and male attributes.

Ellemers, N. (2014). 'Women at work: How organizational features impact career development'. *Policy Insights from Behavioral and Brain Sciences* 1, 1, 46-54.
> This article identifies the social psychological mechanisms that may prevent women from making the same career choices as men.

Frank, R.H. & Cook, P.J. (1996). *The Winner-Take-All Society: Why the Few at the Top Get So Much More Than the Rest of Us.* New York, NY: Penguin Books.
 This book considers growing trends toward income inequality, not just between occupational classes, but also within occupational groups, with certain individuals capturing more lucrative shares.

Inzlicht, M. & Shmader, T. (2011). *Stereotype Threat: Theory, Process, and Application.* New York, NY: Oxford University Press.
 The research summarized in this book suggests that the mere existence of a negative stereotype can lead stigmatized individuals to confirm the stereotype because they worry about confirming the stereotype, which interferes with intellectual performance and academic motivation.

Markus, H.R. & Conner, A. (2013). *Clash! How to Thrive in a Multicultural World.* New York, NY: Penguin Books.
 This book explains that people with different backgrounds have different experiences in society and illustrates how this impacts on their ability to succeed at work.

OECD (2014). *Does Income Inequality Hurt Economic Growth?* Paris: OECD.

Pickett, K. & Vanderbloemen, L. (2015). *Mind the Gap: Tackling Social and Educational Inequality.* York: Cambridge Primary Review Trust.
 This research report reviews evidence on the impact of inequality on childhood, parenting, relationships and family life and assesses policies and initiatives intended to narrow or close the gap between disadvantaged children and the rest.

Tatum, B.D. (1997). *Why Are All the Black Kids Sitting Together in the Cafeteria? And Other Conversations About Race.* New York, NY: Basic Books.

Van Eijk, G. (2010). *Unequal Networks: Spatial Segregation, Relationships and Inequality in the City.* Amsterdam: IOS Press.

Van der Toorn, J., Feinberg, M., Jost, J.T., Kay, A.C., Tyler, T.R., Willer, R. & Wilmuth, C. (2015). 'A sense of powerlessness fosters system justification: Implications for the legitimation of authority, hierarchy, and government'. *Political Psychology* 36, 93-110.
 This article demonstrates how feeling powerless paradoxically leads people to legitimize inequality, thus contributing to their own disadvantage.

Smeeding, T., Erikson, R. & Jänti, M. (eds.) (2011). *Persistence, Privilege, and Parenting: The Comparative Study of Intergenerational Mobility.* New York, NY: Russell Sage.
 This book demonstrates that in many western countries people's socioeconomic status is related to the socioeconomic status of their parents and that intergenerational mobility is more limited than we think.

Van Staveren, I. & Pervaiz, Z. (2015). 'Is it ethnic fractionalization or social exclusion, which affects social cohesion?' *Social Indicators Research* 130, 711-731.
 This article demonstrates that it is social exclusion, which reduces social cohesion, rather than ethnic diversity as such.

Word, C.O., Zanna, M.P. & Cooper, J. (1974). 'The nonverbal mediation of self-fulfilling prophecies in interracial interaction'. *Journal of Experimental Social Psychology* 10, 109-120.
 This article indicates that poor interview performance by stigmatized individuals can be explained by the negative expectations on the part of the non-stigmatized interviewers, which are communicated through non-verbal cues, causing poor performance in response, thus confirming the negative expectations.

Chapter 3: Health

Holt-Lunstad, J., Smith, T.B. & Layton, J.B. (2010). 'Social relationships and mortality risk: A meta-analytic review'. *PLOS Medicine* 7: e1000316. DOI: 10.1371/journal.pmed.1000316.
   Provides a review of 148 studies (including data on over 300,000 individuals) of the relationship between death rates and various measures of friendship. People with good social relationships had only half the risk of death during the follow-up periods than people who were more socially isolated. This was true after taking account of health status at the beginning of the study period, for both sexes, all ages, and involved a reduced risk of many different causes of death.

Jetten, J., Haslam, C. & Haslam, S.A. (eds.) (2012). *The Social Cure: Identity, Health and Well-Being*. New York, NY: Psychology Press.
   Describes how group life and a sense of social identity have a profound impact on general health and well-being.

Jones, C.M. (2010). 'Why should we eliminate health disparities? The moral problem of health disparities'. *Health Policy and Ethics* 100, 47-51.
   Argues that we should work to eliminate health disparities because their existence is a moral wrong that needs to be addressed.

Major, B., Mendes, W.B. & Dovidio, J.F. (2013). 'Intergroup relations and health disparities: A social psychological perspective'. *Health Psychology* 32, 514-524.

Marmot M. (2016). *The Health Gap: The Challenge of an Unequal World*. London: Bloomsbury.

Martire, K.A., Mattick, R.P., Doran, C.M. & Hall, W.D. (2011). 'Cigarette tax and public health: What are the implications of financially stressed smokers for the effects of price increases on smoking prevalence?' *Addiction* 106, 622-630.

Pickett K.E. & Wilkinson R.G. (2008). 'People like us: Ethnic group density effects on health'. *Ethnicity & Health* 13, 321-334.

Ruger, J.P. (2006). 'Ethics and governance of global health inequalities'. *Journal of Epidemiology & Community Health* 60, 998-1003.
   Describes why global health inequalities are morally troubling, why efforts to reduce them are morally justified, and that (inter)national responses to health disparities must be rooted in ethical values because these have the power to motivate, delineate principles, duties and responsibilities.

Sapolsky R. (2005). 'Sick of Poverty'. *Scientific American* 293, 92-99.
   A readable account for the non-specialist of how relative poverty damages health through psychosocial pathways affecting the biology of chronic stress.

Wilkinson, R. & Pickett, K. (2010). *The Spirit Level: Why More Equal Societies Almost Always Do Better*. London: Penguin Books.
   Highlights the damage that inequality does to societies, showing that inequality increases mental and physical health problems in the vast majority of the population, through its effects on status differentiation, our perceptions of how others see us and chronic stress.

Chapter 4: Migration

Bigo, D. & Guild, E. (eds.) (2005). *Controlling Frontiers. Free Movement Into and Within Europe*. Burlington, VT: Ashgate Publishing Limited.
A respected and wide-ranging collection of essays on issues that arise with the migration of individuals both into and within Europe.

Carens, J.H. (2013). *The Ethics of Immigration*. Oxford: Oxford University Press.
Two decades ago, Carens was the first to point out that, within liberal societies, the right to free movement is considered an important individual freedom, and yet we take it for granted that states have the right to restrict movement across national borders. He argued, on this basis, that liberals should be committed to 'open borders'. In The Ethics of Immigration, Carens considers how this utopian vision, of a world in which immigration is a right, not a privilege, can nevertheless guide out thinking about many of the concrete policy questions that arise in the world that we live in.

De Swaan, A. (1995). 'Widening circles of identification: Emotional concerns in sociogenetic perspective'. *Theory, Culture, & Society* 12, 25-39.
Describes how throughout the development of the human kind, identification with broader circles of identification emerged (from the family to local community, to the nation state and other social categories).

Gaertner, S.L., Dovidio, J.F. & Bachman, B. (1996). 'Revisiting the contact hypothesis: The induction of a common ingroup identity'. *International Journal of Intercultural Relations* 20, 271-290.
Describes the common in-group model, i.e., the idea that in order to reduce prejudice between specific in-groups and out-groups one should tress the common identity they share at a higher level of self-definition, as well as the possibility of a dual identity, i.e., identifying with the in-group as well as the overarching social identity.

Hainmueller, J. & Hopkins, D.J. (2014). 'Public attitudes toward immigration'. *Annual Review of Political Science* 17, 225-249.
Provides evidence that negative attitudes towards migration are not so much due to personal economic circumstances, but to concerns about cultural clashes, and to a lesser extend economic implications at the national level.

Kleingeld, P. (2012). *Kant and Cosmopolitanism: The Philosophical Ideal of World Citizenship*. Cambridge: Cambridge University Press.

Kleingeld, P. & Brown, E. (2014). 'Cosmopolitanism'. In: Edward N. Zalta (ed.), *The Stanford Encyclopedia of Philosophy* (Fall 2014 edition). Online: https://plato.stanford.edu/archives/fall2014/entries/cosmopolitanism

MacKenzie, D. (2016). 'On the road again'. *New Scientist* 230 (3068), 29-37.
Sketches the historical trends and current magnitude of worldwide migration, and discusses the economic implications.

Nussbaum, M.C. (1997). 'Kant and Stoic Cosmopolitanism'. *The Journal of Political Philosophy* 1, 1-25.
Describes the stoic position on cosmopolitism. Whereas classic stoic philosophy sees human beings as just 'citizens of the world', later elaborations focus on ties with both the global community and one's birthplace community (polis).

Rosenmann, A., Reese, G. & Cameron, J.E. (2016). 'Social Identities in a globalized world: Challenges and opportunities for collective action'. *Perspectives on Psychological Science* 11, 202-221.
Describes the psychological possibility and consequences of forming an identity on a global level.

Smith, P.K. & Trope, Y. (2006). 'You focus on the forest when you're in charge of the trees: Power priming and abstract information processing'. *Journal of Personality and Social Psychology* 90, 578-596.
Construal level theory describes two ways of perceiving the world: More abstractly (globally) terms and more concretely (locally). Low power people and groups tend to perceive the world using a more local mindset while high power people and groups tend to perceive the world using a more global mindset.

Stephan, W. G., & Ybarra, O., & Rios Morrison, K. (2009). Stephan, W.G., & Ybarra, O. & Rios Morrison, K. (2009). 'Intergroup Threat Theory'. In: T.D. Nelson (ed.), *Handbook of Prejudice, Stereotyping, and Discrimination*. New York, NY: Psychology Press.
  Describes integrated threat theory, making a distinction between three forms of threat in inter-group contexts: realistic (economic) threats, symbolic (identity) threats and inter-group anxiety.

Chapter 5: Climate change

Baer, P., Athanasiou, T., Kartha, S. & Kemp-Benedict, E. (2008). *The Greenhouse Development Rights Framework: The Right to Development in a Climate Constrained World* (2nd ed.). Berlin and Albany, CA: Heinrich Böll Foundation, Christian Aid, EcoEquity and the Stockholm Environment Institute. Online: www.greenhousedevelopmentrights.org.

Bain, P.G., Milfont, T.L., Kashima, Y., Bilewicz, M., Doron, G., Gardarsdottir, R.B. et al. & Saviolidis, N.M. (2016). 'Co-benefits of addressing climate change can motivate action around the world'. *Nature Climate Change* 6, 154-157.
  Describes a study revealing that people across the world are more likely to support climate policies when they realize that a society that cares for the environment is a society of committed and involved people.

Bolderdijk, J.W., Steg, L., Geller, E.S., Lehman, P.K. & Postmes, T. (2013). 'Comparing the effectiveness of monetary versus moral motives in environmental campaigning'. *Nature Climate Change* 3, 413-416.
  Psychological study that demonstrates that moral motives are a more important determinant of environmental behaviours than monetary motives.

Clayton, S., Devine-Wright, P., Swim, J., Bonnes, M., Steg, L., Whitmarsh, L. & Carrico, A. (2016). 'Expanding the role for psychology in addressing environmental challenges'. *American Psychologist* 71, 199-215.
  Clear explanation of the role that psychological research can play in the public debate on climate change.

Doorn, N. (2017). 'Resilience indicators: Opportunities for including distributive justice concerns in disaster management'. *Journal of Risk Research*. DOI:10.1080/1366 9877.2015.1100662.
  This paper presents a systematic review of the concept of resilience in the field of disaster management, with a focus how distributive justice considerations are included. The analysis shows that , although recognized as important, distributive issues are not currently addressed in the context of resilience and disaster management.

Doorn, N. (2013). 'Water and justice: To-wards and ethics of water governance'. *Public Reason* 5, 95-111.
Water is recognized to pose some very urgent questions in the near future. A significant number of people are deprived of clean drinking water and sanitation services. At the same time, an increasing percentage of the global population lives in areas that are at risk of flooding, partly exacerbated by climate change. In this paper, it is argued that political philosophers or applied ethicists should become more involved in the debate on water governance in order to (1) clarify the debate; and (2) help analyzing some urgent distributive questions related to water governance.

Frey, B.S. & Jegen, R. (2001). 'Motivation Crowding Theory'. *Journal of Economic Surveys* 15, 589-611.
Shows that extrinsic rewards (such as monetary incentives) can reduce the motivation to behave in environmentally friendly ways.

Gardiner, S.M. (2011). *A Perfect Moral Storm: The Ethical Tragedy of Climate Change.* Oxford: Oxford University Press.

Gardiner, S.M. (2014). 'A call for a global constitutional convention focused on future generations'. *Ethics and International Affairs* 28, 299-315.

Klein, N. (2014). *This Changes Everything. Capitalism vs. The Climate/No Time. Verander nu voor het klimaat alles verandert.*

London: Penguin/Amsterdam: De Geus.
Mitchell, D. (2008). 'A Note on Rising Food Prices'. *World Bank Policy Research Working Paper No 4682.* Washington, DC: The World Bank. Online: www.http://elibrary.worldbank.org/doi/abs/10.1596/1813-9450-4682.

Roeser, S. (2012). 'Risk communication, moral emotions and climate change'. *Risk Analysis* 32, 1033-1040.
This article discusses the potential role that emotions might play in enticing a lifestyle that diminishes climate change.

Roeser, S. (2006). 'The role of emotions in judging the moral acceptability of risks'. *Safety Science* 44, 689-700.
This paper argues that we need emotions in order to make a rational decision as to the moral acceptability of technological risks.

Storm, S. (2009). 'Capitalism and climate change: Can the invisible hand adjust the natural thermostat?' *Development and Change* 40, 1011-1038.

Storm, S. (2016). 'How the invisible hand is supposed to adjust the natural thermostat: A guide for the perplexed'. *Science and Engineering Ethics.* DOI 10.1007/s11948-016-9780-3.

Illustration credits

p. 15: Kostis Ntantamis/Zuma Press/Hollandse Hoogte
p. 16: Look Bildagentur der Fotografen/Hollandse Hoogte
p. 20: Ye Pingfan Xinhua/Eyevine/Hollandse Hoogte
p. 25: Roger Dohmen/Hollandse Hoogte
p. 35: Rink Hof/Hollandse Hoogte
p. 38: Sand Xinhua/Eyevine/Hollandse Hoogte
p. 47: Piet den Blanken/Hollandse Hoogte
p. 49: Theo Audenaerd/Hollandse Hoogte
p. 52: Rob Huibers/Hollandse Hoogte
p. 56, 57: Caspar Huurdeman/Hollandse Hoogte
p. 62: Berlinda van Dam/Hollandse Hoogte
p. 66: Klaas Fopma/Hollandse Hoogte
p. 69: Hans van Rhoon/Hollandse Hoogte
p. 74: Berlinda van Dam/Hollandse Hoogte
p. 81: Bert Spiertz/Hollandse Hoogte
p. 82: Peter de Krom/Hollandse Hoogte
p. 89: Jaco Klamer/Hollandse Hoogte
p. 93: Joost van den Broek/Hollandse Hoogte
p. 97: Marcel van den Bergh/Hollandse Hoogte
p. 98, 99: Guido Koppes/GFK/Hollandse Hoogte
p. 104: Martijn de Jonge/Hollandse Hoogte
p. 108: BELGA/Photo Benoit Doppagne/Hollandse Hoogte
p. 112: Jochem Wijnands/Hollandse Hoogte
p. 117: Leonie Pauw/Hollandse Hoogte
p. 125: Flip Franssen/Hollandse Hoogte